Wiggle, Giggle & Shake
200 Ways to Move and Learn

Rae Pica

Illustrations: Katheryn Davis

Dedication

This book is dedicated to my two dearest friends, Sheila Chapman and Patti Page, with deepest thanks for their "life support."

Wiggle Giggle & Shake

200 Ways to Move and Learn

Rae Pica

gryphon house®, inc.
Beltsville, MD

Copyright

Portions of this book were previously published in 1991 as *Special Themes for Moving
and Learning.*

Library of Congress Cataloging-in-Publication Data

Pica, Rae, 1953–
    Wiggle, giggle and shake: 200 ways to move and learn / Rae Pica ; illustrations,
Katheryn Davis.
        p. cm.
    Rev. ed. of: Special themes for moving & learning. c1991.
    Includes index.
    ISBN13: 978-087659-244-1
    ISBN10: 0-87659-244-2
    1. Movement education. I. Title: 200 ways to move and learn. II. Pica, Rae, 1953–
Special themes for moving & learning. III. Title.

    GV452.P525 2001
    372.86--dc21

                                                                          2001033344

Illustrations: Katheryn Davis
Cover photograph: ©2001 Walter Larrimore.

Bulk purchase

Gryphon House books are available at special discount when purchased in bulk for
    special premiums and sales promotions as well as for fund-raising use. Special
    editions or book excerpts also can be created to specification. For details,
    contact the Director of Sales at the address above.

Disclaimer

The publisher and the author cannot be held responsible for injury, mishap, or
    damages incurred during the use of or because of the activities in this book. The
    author recommends appropriate and reasonable supervision at all times based
    on the age and capability of each child.

Table of Contents

Wiggle, Giggle, and Shake is filled with ideas for exploring classroom themes through movement. Why? Because through movement experiences, abstract concepts become more concrete. Because when children physically experience a concept, it is far more likely to make a long-lasting impression. Because if we're to truly address the whole child, we must recognize children as thinking, feeling, moving human beings!

Originally published in 1991 as *Special Themes for Moving & Learning,* this new version, like the first, explores popular classroom themes with the whole child in mind. The movement activities in *Wiggle, Giggle, and Shake* challenge children to think and solve problems, to recognize and explore their feelings, and to physically participate in their own learning. Because the activities offer a multimodal approach to learning, the knowledge is "imprinted" in the children's minds and bodies. As Confucius said so many years ago, "What I hear, I forget. What I see, I remember. What I do, I know." *Wiggle, Giggle, and Shake* offers children opportunities to do and know.

MOVEMENT'S ROLE IN LEARNING

Movement is an important element in programs for young children. It promotes physical fitness and development of the whole child, and it contributes to the enhancement of a positive self-image, self-confidence, creativity, and self-expression. Furthermore, movement stimulates the learning process. There is increasing evidence that because a child's earliest learning is based on motor development, subsequent learning is too.

Early childhood professionals have long known that young children learn experientially—through play, experimentation, exploration, and discovery. And now researchers in the field of neuroscience are verifying it, having confirmed that the brain actually changes as a result of experience (Shore, 1997). Brain cells (called neurons) are stimulated by sensory experiences, thus producing more connections (synapses) to other brain cells. These synapses are critical to learning, and if they're not to be "weeded out," they must continue to receive stimulation; it's very much a use-it-or-lose-it situation. Thus, for children's brains to function optimally, they must have active experiences that produce and strengthen these brain connections.

This is truly an exciting time to be a teacher, a child, or a movement specialist—as more and more brain research is pointing to the link between moving and learning. Neurophysiologist Carla Hannaford (1995) tells us, among other things, that:
- "movement activates the neural wiring throughout the body, making the whole body the instrument of learning" (p. 13);
- beginning in infancy and continuing throughout our lives, physical movement plays an essential role in creating nerve cell networks that are the essence of learning (p. 12); and
- in studies where children spent extra time in daily physical activity, they showed a higher level of academic success (pp. 101, 106-7).

In his groundbreaking work, developmental psychologist Howard Gardner (1981) has determined that intelligence is not a singular entity that can be tested only with paper and pencil. Rather, he contends that we each possess eight different kinds of intelligence, to greater or lesser degrees, and in varying combinations. And he has designated the bodily/kinesthetic as an intelligence, asserting that individuals can learn and know with their bodies or body parts. Movement, of course, promotes development of the bodily/kinesthetic intelligence. It enhances spatial intelligence, too, and can also help develop the musical, logical/mathematical, linguistic, interpersonal, and intrapersonal intelligences. That's seven of the eight intelligences Gardner has identified!

Finally, Fauth (1990, p. 160) lends credence to the belief that children are better served by multimodal learning. She tells us that we retain:

- 10 percent of what we read;
- 20 percent of what we hear;
- 30 percent of what we see;
- 50 percent of what we hear and see at the same time;
- 70 percent of what we hear, see, and say; and
- 90 percent of what we hear, see, say, and do.

Though the functions of the mind have long been considered superior to the functions of the body, today's research demands that we re-think that position and begin to look at the mind and body as united. As Hannaford (1995, p. 16) maintains, "We have spent years and resources struggling to teach people to learn, and yet the standardized achievement test scores go down and illiteracy rises. Could it be that one of the key elements we've been missing is simply movement?"

HOW TO USE THIS BOOK

Wiggle, Giggle, and Shake is written for teachers of children ages 4 to 8 (preschool through second grade). It is for those teachers who want the children in their class to explore and discover and construct their own knowledge, and to physically experience concepts and to do so creatively. It's for those who sometimes do movement, those who regularly do movement, and even those who've never done movement! It's for anyone looking for an infusion of new ideas. In short, it's for everyone who believes in the whole child.

If you're concerned you may not know enough about movement to make it part of the children's education, don't be! Movement is something that's familiar to all of us! And with *Wiggle, Giggle, and Shake*, movement is especially easy. This book offers simple, practical, and fun movement activities and ideas grouped according to popular classroom themes. They are easily usable whether or not you have experience in movement education.

I've carefully selected the 40 themes in the book based on my study of a number of other activity books, as well as discussions with many early childhood and elementary teaching professionals. For every theme, there are five principal activities, giving you 200 activities from which to choose—easily a full year's worth! Although the holidays and seasons appear in the book according to their order in the school year, the activities themselves are not arranged in any particular order. You may choose to use some or all of the five activities at one time, perhaps as part of a movement session. Or you can use one activity per day, making movement a daily part of your study of a unit. And, certainly, you can also refer to *Wiggle, Giggle, and Shake* when in need of a transition, a time-filler, or a motivator.

Some of the activities require little space and, therefore, are great to use at Circle Time. Others suggest variations intended to extend an activity or to provide additional ideas for future exploration. A bit of advance planning is needed for some of the activities, such as choosing a piece of music or putting words or pictures on scraps of paper that the children will draw from a hat or box. In addition, some of the activities can be completed in just a few minutes, while others may require more time or several repetitions before they can be accomplished successfully.

My suggestion is that you first look at the themes covered in *Wiggle, Giggle, and Shake*. Then, by simply selecting in advance the activity or activities you want to explore with the children, you can ensure there won't be any last-minute glitches. For example, if you are exploring occupations one week and want to concentrate on homemaking, you can see in the table of contents that the topic is covered in the theme Keeping House in Chapter 8. The next step is to determine how many activities you want to perform on a particular day. For example, if you know that you'll only have time for one activity, decide ahead of time which of the five activities you will do. Review the activity to see if you need any particular materials. If you choose the activity "A Dusting Dance," for example, a glance at the section entitled "Before" alerts you to have some pieces of cloth for the children to use.

Of course, you know the children in your class better than I do, so you will need to determine if they're going to require more help than what I've suggested with the activities. For instance, if an activity requires children to draw words from a container and some of the children are not able to read yet, you may choose instead to put pictures or colors on the paper scraps, or you can read the words for the children. You may also find that with some activities, you have to provide more verbal assistance for the children. For example, in the activity "The Bank Teller" (under the theme More Professions in Chapter 8), different dollar amounts are represented by different movement skills. If some of the children have trouble remembering the correlations, there's no reason why you simply can't tell them!

For the most part, there's very little work involved in using this book. A number of teachers have told me how difficult it is to implement some movement activities due to the materials and equipment required, so I've purposely created activities that require few or no props. In addition, those props that are required are items found in a typical classroom.

Basically, all that will be required of you (in addition to a bit of advance preparation) is the presentation of the challenges suggested for each activity. I will go over that in the following section.

THE TEACHER'S ROLE

Teachers often ask me whether or not they should participate with the children. And my answer is, "Yes and no." Some of the activities in *Wiggle, Giggle, and Shake* are clearly teacher-directed, such as "Follow the Leader" (page 42) and "Mirror Game" (page 17). These activities require you to move right along with the children because imitation is the intended goal! When this is the case, the more fun you have, the more the children will enjoy the activity. Teacher-directed activities also offer important learning objectives for the children, such as following directions and trying to physically replicate what the eyes are seeing.

Most of the activities, however, employ movement exploration (or divergent problem solving) as a teaching method. This means that while you'll be presenting the challenges and facilitating the learning, the responses themselves will be child-directed. In other words, because there will be many possible responses to every single challenge, you shouldn't demonstrate the "answers" yourself.

For example, the children will each have individual and often unique interpretations to challenges such as how to look like a potato being mashed, move like a bear crossing a fallen tree trunk, or pretend to be feeling mad. If you were to demonstrate these actions, they would most likely imitate you. However, if you encourage them to show you how they would be or do any of these things and positively react to all the different solutions they demonstrate, they will be encouraged to continue finding creative responses. They'll be thinking, feeling, and moving!

Your "job" for most of the activities found in this book is simply to prepare any required materials, lead a discussion about the topic being explored, and then present the challenges involved. Of course, you will want to do so with the appropriate vocal and facial expressions and lots of enthusiasm!

CLASSROOM MANAGEMENT

The potential for children "bouncing off the walls" is a concern when it comes to movement. Often, it's even an impediment to doing movement! To address the issue, I dedicated an entire chapter of my textbook, *Experiences in Movement,* to creating and maintaining a positive learning environment (Pica, 2000). I've even conducted workshops on the subject, called "Maintaining Discipline—and Sanity—with Kids on the Move." Obviously, this book isn't the place for an entire chapter's or workshop's worth of information. But, since I want you to take full advantage of movement's many benefits, and to enjoy using the activities in this book, I'm offering a few suggestions here to help you keep children off the walls!

First and foremost, make it a goal for the children to avoid colliding or interfering with one another. You can do this by asking the children to space themselves evenly at the start of every movement session (or activity) and then continually reinforcing the concept of personal space. For example, you can encourage the children to imagine they're each surrounded by a giant bubble, which they must avoid bursting by not getting too close to one another.

Also, establish a signal to indicate that it is time to stop, look, and listen. Choose a signal the children have to watch for while moving (for example, two fingers held in the air or the time-out sign from sports) or something they must listen for (for example, a hand clap, a strike on a triangle, or two taps on a drum). If using the latter, make sure your signal is a quiet one so the children have to be quiet enough to hear it. The goal is to have the children stop, look, and listen within two to five seconds. Keep in mind that you will have to practice this if they're to meet the goal.

If the children occasionally demonstrate disruptive behavior, ignoring it is often the best way to get it to stop. If, however, the behavior is harmful to the child or to others, ignoring it is not a possibility. You should then handle the situation as you would at any other time disruptive behavior is an issue, such as a time-out, a visit to the problem-solving table, or any other method you typically employ.

If, at the other extreme, you have children who don't participate at all in the movement activities, you should first determine why they choose to sit out. Is it due to a physical problem? Are they simply shy? Or are they using nonparticipation as a way to get your attention?

If you determine that the child is trying to get your attention, ignoring him is your best bet. Offer reinforcement only when the child participates in group activities. If the child is indeed shy, he may just need time to get used to the idea of moving with the rest of the group, or he may respond to a bit of gentle encouragement. Sometimes merely standing near the shy child as you facilitate movement activities, offering occasional smiles or gentle touches, is the only encouragement you need to offer. At other times, you may have to physically (but gently) initiate the child's participation by taking his hands in yours and moving them accordingly, or sitting behind the child and rocking him with you to the rhythm of the music. Positively reinforcing any level of participation can also do much to contribute to the shy child's confidence. For example, if you've asked the children to make a "gentle" movement and the shy child blinks, you can use his "response" as an example.

Whatever the reason for the child's lack of involvement, forcing participation will only incur undue emotional stress. Instead, ask nonparticipants to take on the role of audience. This involves them to a certain extent and ensures they are gaining something from the experience, as they can absorb a lot from watching movement take place.

Generally speaking, you should have few management problems as you move through the activities in *Wiggle, Giggle, and Shake*. Because the activities lend themselves to success, the children experiencing success are too absorbed to want to wreak havoc!

NEW TO THIS EDITION

As mentioned earlier, each activity includes a section entitled "Before," which alerts you to any materials or music you may need for an activity. This is also the section that provides background information on the topic and suggestions for what you should discuss with the children before getting to the heart of the activity (entitled "During").

Also new to this edition is the section following each activity. Appropriately entitled "After," this section proposes ideas for connecting the movement activity to other areas of the curriculum. Included are suggestions for books, recordings, art projects, field trips, and more—all of which relate in some way to the movement activity explored. Remember, they are only suggestions. You probably know of other suitable books or recordings that you will want to use. My ideas for follow-up activities will most likely spark some of your own ideas. The important point to remember is that these suggestions are intended to enhance the exploration of a particular topic so the children truly experience a multimodal, whole-child approach to learning.

I've also added two themes to *Wiggle, Giggle, and Shake* that weren't in the original edition. The first is Kwanzaa, which is in Holidays and Celebrations (Chapter 4). My intention was to provide teachers with diverse possibilities for exploring the many family celebrations that occur during the month of December (Christmas, Hanukkah, and Kwanzaa). It is my hope that in addition to using the activities for each of these three holidays, teachers will point out the many similarities among the three.

The other new theme is Creatures and Critters, which is in Fun Themes (Chapter 10). It includes explorations of giants and elves, dinosaurs, insects and arachnids, fairies, and teddy bears. Children love these things!

I hope you enjoy the activities in this book as much as the children do. I firmly believe that regardless of our age, we should never stop moving and learning!

REFERENCES

Fauth, B. (1990). Linking the visual arts with drama, movement, and dance for the young child. In W.J. Stinson, ed., *Moving and learning for the young child* (pp. 159-87). Reston VA: American Alliance for Health, Physical Education, Recreation, and Dance.

Gardner, H. (1993). *Frames of mind: The theory of multiple intelligences.* New York: Basic Books.

Hannaford, C. (1995). *Smart moves: Why learning is not all in your head.* Arlington VA: Great Ocean Publishers.

Pica, R. (2000). *Experiences in movement,* 2nd ed. Albany NY: Delmar.

Shore, R. (1997). *Rethinking the brain: New insights into early development.* New York: Families and Work Institute.

Self-Awareness

CHAPTER ONE

BODY PARTS

Learning Objectives
• *To identify body parts and enhance body awareness*

BEFORE

◀ The traditional game of Simon Says can be a wonderful body parts identification activity, except for the fact that its rules eliminate children—and those who need to participate the most are usually the first to go!

◀ Show Me is simply Simon Says without elimination. (If some children respond "incorrectly," you can always enthusiastically point out some of the other children's responses so they have a chance to adjust accordingly.)

◀ Some children will be confused by the fact that there's no elimination, so you'll need to make it clear to them that this game is different!

DURING

◀ Instead of beginning your request with "Simon Says," say, "Show me..." Ask the children to show you how they do the following:
  • Bend their knees
  • Blink their eyes
  • Cover their ears
  • Give themselves a hug
  • Nod their heads
  • Pat their tummies
  • Pucker their mouths
  • Put their hands on their hips
  • Squeeze their elbows
  • Stand on one foot
  • Touch their shoulders
  • Touch their toes
  • Wave their hands
  • Wiggle their fingers
  • Wiggle their noses

ALSO

◀ If you want to promote listening skills, ask the children to arrange themselves into two different circles or lines prior to starting.

◀ Then, if some children move without first hearing the words, "Show me," they simply go from one circle or line to the other. This way, they will need to listen carefully but can still keep participating.

◀ Once the children become adept at locating the above body parts, challenge them with other body parts, such as foreheads, temples, wrists, ankles, and shins!

AFTER

• *Full-size poster of a child, preferably with labeled body parts*

◀ Hang a full-size poster of a child's body on the wall so the children have another way to identify body parts. A poster with labeled body parts is best.

WIGGLE, GIGGLE, AND SHAKE

Mirror Game

BEFORE

◄ This game is similar to Show Me (page 16), except you will be giving the children visual cues instead of verbal ones.

◄ Verbal cues enhance listening skills. The Mirror Game, however, develops visual awareness because the children will physically imitate what they see.

◄ Talk to the children about mirrors and how they reflect images. Where in their homes do they have mirrors? What kinds of activities might they perform while looking in a mirror?

DURING

◄ Stand and face the children in a spot where they all have a clear view of you.

◄ Ask them to imagine that they're looking into a mirror and that you are their reflection. This means that they must do exactly what they see you do.

◄ Silently perform many of the same movements from Show Me. Because most of these are static poses or simple movements, the children will soon get the hang of it. (Move slowly when changing from one position to the next!)

ALSO

◄ For more challenge, perform movements such as hopping or jumping in place (or from side to side), waving your arms, shaking the body or various body parts, and so on.

AFTER

• *Full-size unbreakable mirror*

◄ Bring in a full-size mirror and encourage the children to take turns making a variety of shapes in front of it.

◄ Encourage them to explore a variety of body parts, with both sides of their bodies and at different levels in space (high, low, and in the middle).

My Face Can Say...

BEFORE

◄ Discuss body language with the children. Explain that sometimes we can express what we're feeling or what we want to say with no words at all. The face, being the most expressive body part we have, is very capable of doing just that!

DURING

◄ Ask the children to show you how they would express the following using only their faces:
  - I'm tired.
  - I'm mad.
  - I'm afraid.
  - That tastes yummy.
  - That tastes yucky.
  - I'm sad.
  - That smells good.
  - That smells awful.
  - What a surprise!
  - I'm happy!

AFTER
- **Unbreakable hand-held mirrors**
- **Art materials, such as paper, markers, paint, scissors, and glue**

◄ Provide each child with an unbreakable hand-held mirror and a variety of art materials, including paints and markers in many different skin shades.
◄ Encourage them to each create a self-portrait (their faces only).

My Hands Can Say...

BEFORE

◄ Explain to the children that, like our faces, our hands can also "say" many things for us. What are some of the times the children have felt hot, cold, mad, or scared?

DURING

◄ Ask the children to show you, using only their hands, how they would express the following:
  - Hello!
  - Come here.
  - Go away.
  - Naughty, naughty.
  - I'm hot.

- I'm scared.
- Stop!
- I'm mad.
- I'm cold.
- Goodbye!
- Yea!

AFTER

◄ You can use this opportunity to discuss emotions such as anger and fear, which are usually considered "negative."

◄ Assure the children that all feelings are valid.

◄ If you are familiar with sign language, this would be a great time to introduce it to the children to show them a different way of "talking with our hands!"

The Body Poem

BEFORE

◄ Before doing any activity, read the following poem to the children so they know what to expect.

◄ In addition to the parts mentioned in the poem, what other body parts do the children have more than one of? How many of each? How many teeth and hairs do they think they have?

DURING

◄ Explain to the children that you are going to read "The Body Poem" again. This time, however, they should touch or display the appropriate body parts as they are mentioned in the poem.

◄ For the last segment, they should shrug their shoulders when you read, "So why, do you suppose." Then, they should move their hands from the top of their body to the bottom when you read the next two lines.

The Body Poem
I have two feet,
Two ears, two legs,
Ten fingers and ten toes;
I have two knees,
Two lips, two hands,
And even two elbows.

I have two eyes
And four eyelids.
So why, do you suppose,
With all these parts
On my body
I only have one nose?!

ALSO

◄ The children should perform the activity slowly at first, but as they become more familiar with the poem (and are even reciting it themselves), they'll have lots of fun if you do it faster each time.

◄ Once they're thoroughly familiar with it, you might want to introduce them to the concept of *accelerando,* which means beginning very slowly and then gradually speaking faster and faster. Begin the poem slowly, then speak faster and faster as you recite the lines so that it actually ends in a rush!

AFTER
• Two Eyes, a Nose, and a Mouth *by Roberta Grovel Intrater*

◄ Read *Two Eyes, a Nose, and a Mouth* by Roberta Grovel Intrater to the children.

Tasting

THE SENSES

Learning Objectives
- *To inspire children to consider the five senses*
- *To foster appreciation for the functions of the five senses*

BEFORE
- Talk to the children about their favorite foods and the way they taste.
- How do those tastes make them feel? What tastes don't they like? Why?
- Discuss the tastes mentioned below. Ask the children to describe how each of the tastes makes them feel.

DURING
- First, assure the children that not all of the following tastes will make them react in the same way. Then challenge them to show you, with their faces only, how each taste makes them feel:
  - A sour lemon
  - A very bubbly drink
  - Salty potato chips
  - Spicy food (such as a hot pepper)
  - Hot chocolate
  - A pickle
  - Peanut butter
  - Ice cream (their favorite flavor)

ALSO
- An alternative is to ask the children to demonstrate with their whole bodies what the above tastes bring to mind.

AFTER
- *A variety of foods to taste*

- Use this activity as an opportunity to discuss sweet, sour, salty, and bitter tastes, or the food groups to which some of the above items belong.
- If possible, bring in some of the items listed and have a tasting party!

Smelling

BEFORE
- Like tasting, smelling different things can create a variety of reactions in us.
- Talk to the children about how the various odors listed below make them feel.
- What are their favorite smells? Why?

DURING
- This activity is similar to Tasting (previous activity). However, this time the children will show you with their whole bodies (or the appropriate body parts) how certain odors make them feel. Odors can include:

- Sour milk
- Cookies baking
- A skunk
- A clean, crisp day
- Onions
- A rose (or other flowers)

AFTER

◀ The senses fall under the content area of science.

◀ Continue your exploration of the sense of smell by bringing the children outdoors and challenging them to find or gather items with strong scents.

◀ Ask them to describe these scents. How do these scents make them feel like moving?

Hearing

BEFORE

- **Objects that make noise (see list below)**

◀ Gather a variety of noisemakers (see examples below).

◀ Talk to the children about all the various sounds they might hear during the course of a day. You might ask:
- Do you hear different sounds at home than you do at school?
- What sounds are pleasant to hear?
- Which sounds do you find unpleasant? Why?

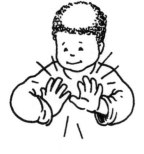

DURING

◀ Ask the children to move however each of the following sounds makes them feel like moving. Try making these sounds (or other sounds):
- Strike pots and pans
- Ring a bell
- Blow a whistle
- Shake a coffee can partially filled with sand
- Separate Velcro tabs
- Lightly strike a glass with a spoon
- Crumple a piece of paper
- Tap a desk with a ruler

ALSO

◀ In lieu of noisemakers, try using only body sounds. In addition to clapping and stamping, you might whistle, click your tongue, snap your fingers, smack your lips, "drum" a thigh, or inhale and exhale loudly.

AFTER

◀ In the Music Center, frequently introduce new objects that make sounds (not only instruments, but also environmental items, gadgets, and tools) to foster children's creativity and keep them interested in producing new sounds.

Touching

BEFORE

◄ Touch is probably the sense that we most take for granted. A smell or a sound can draw our full attention and even invoke memories of times gone by. A beautiful sight (or a startling one) causes us to pause and take notice and forms a lasting impression in the mind. Tasting often provides some of our most pleasurable daily sensations. But things that we touch usually make less of an impression (unless we are consciously stroking a cat's fur, for instance, or are burned by a hot stove). For example, we pick up a toothbrush without noticing the smoothness of the handle, put on our clothes without registering the feel of the cloth, and close a door without really feeling the shape and texture of the doorknob.

◄ Talk to the children about such daily events. Ask them to describe the feel of some of the objects they commonly touch. Mention items of varying textures, such as a glass, a "scratchy" sweater, warm water, or a pencil.

◄ Then, ask the children to look around the room and point out some of the different textures they find.

DURING
• Two pieces of music, one soft and one upbeat

◄ Choose two pieces of music, one soft and slow and the other upbeat.

◄ Play one of the pieces of music and ask the children to move or dance around the room, patting and stroking lots of different textures.

◄ Do the items that they touch make them feel like moving in different ways?

◄ Now play the second piece of music and ask the children to perform the "touching dance" again.

◄ Does this style of the music inspire them to touch things in different ways?

◄ Finally, briefly repeat the activity without any music at all. How does this affect the children's responses?

AFTER
• Objects with a variety of textures and a large box

◄ Further explore the concept of texture, which falls under the content areas of art and science, by gathering items with different textures and placing them in a large box. (Possibilities include such varying textures as burlap, silk, a feather, a teddy bear, and a marble.)

◄ Ask the children, one at a time, to reach into the box and touch only one item.

◄ Can they identify what they're feeling?

◄ As an extension, challenge the children to show you with their bodies how the item makes them feel like moving. A feather, for example, might prompt "ticklish" movement, while burlap might inspire scratching.

BEFORE

◄ Ask the children what the most beautiful sights are that they have seen.
  - What do they see when they first open their eyes in the morning?
  - What are their favorite colors? Why?
  - What faraway place would they like to see someday?
◄ This kind of question helps the children begin to think about the sense of sight.

DURING

◄ In this exercise, the children are going to consider sight by experiencing its opposite: sightlessness. Explain to them that now that they have talked about seeing lots of things, they're going to discover what it's like to do some things *without* seeing.

◄ Begin by asking the children to each sit in their own personal space (see page 11 in the Introduction). Then ask them to close their eyes.

◄ Do they feel any different? (These questions don't necessarily require a verbal response from the children; rather, they are asked to encourage the children to consider what they're experiencing.)

◄ Ask them to briefly open their eyes to reorient themselves, and then close their eyes again and stand up (keeping their eyes closed).

◄ Once standing, ask the children to open their eyes for a moment (they should always do this momentarily between activities) and then close them again.

◄ Does standing with their eyes closed feel different?

◄ Continue this process, cueing the children to experience the differences with their eyes open and then closed when doing the following:
  - Standing on tiptoe
  - Standing (flat-footed) on one foot
  - Standing (briefly) on one foot on tiptoe
  - Standing flat-footed and leaning, alternately, in all four directions; repeat on tiptoe
  - Taking a few steps forward, backward, and to either side

AFTER

◄ To develop listening skills in early childhood, teachers and caregivers often use what are called *focused* or *active* listening experiences. So, how about using focused, or active, *seeing* experiences?

◄ Bring the children outdoors and ask them, one at a time, to name something they see.

◄ You'll probably be amazed at how much they notice when you make a game out of it.

◄ If it's a sunny day with some friendly clouds in the sky, ask the children to sit or lie on the ground and look up at the clouds. Encourage them to find all the shapes or creatures they can identify.

Feeling Sad

Learning Objectives
• To encourage children to consider and accept their feelings
• To promote self-expression

BEFORE

• Slow, sad piece of music

◄ Choose a soft, slow, and if possible, sad piece of music for this activity. (Samuel Barber's *Adagio for Strings* is a perfect example, but there are many instrumental numbers, often found on recordings used for quiet times, that would also be appropriate.)

◄ Discuss sadness with the children, asking for examples of times they've felt sad. Ask them:

• How did your faces and bodies look when you were feeling sad?
• How did you move? Did you move quickly or slowly? "Bouncy" or "dragging?"

DURING

◄ Play the piece of music you selected and ask the children to show you how their faces look when they're sad.

◄ Continue with the following questions:

• How do you walk when you're sad?
• How could you show me with your hands and arms that you're sad?
• Make up a "sad dance" to this music.
• Show me how you're sad in a sitting position. How about lying down?

AFTER

• Let's Talk About Feeling Sad *by Joy Wilt Berry*

◄ Assure the children that it's okay to feel sad sometimes—everybody does.

◄ Read and discuss *Let's Talk About Feeling Sad* by Joy Wilt Berry.

Feeling Mad

BEFORE

◄ Anger is an emotion with which all children are familiar, and they need to be assured that it's legitimate. It's okay to feel mad, as long as they don't hurt themselves or someone else.

◄ Also, just like other emotions, anger requires expression. Ask the children:

• What are some of the ways people might express their anger?
• Which ways are "positive" and which are "negative?"

◄ In your discussion, be sure to mention the forms of expression mentioned in the following poem.

DURING

◄ Ask the children to act out the lines of this poem:

Feeling Mad

I clench my fists
And raise them high.
I stomp my feet real loud.
I walk around with shoulders hunched;
My face, it has a scowl.

I kick the floor
And scuff my feet.
I'm acting really "bad";
But I can't help the way I feel
Because, you see, I'm mad!

AFTER

• I Was So Mad! by Norma Simon or Feeling Angry by Joy Wilt Berry

◄ At the end of the poem, ask the children to shake out all their anger and then give themselves a great big hug!

◄ Then, read Norma Simon's *I Was So Mad* or *Feeling Angry* by Joy Wilt Berry to the children.

Feeling Scared

BEFORE

◄ Fear is one emotion that many people, both young and old, don't like to admit to. But again, like any other emotion, it's perfectly legitimate to feel fear at times.

◄ Ask the children, "When are some times when you might feel scared?"

DURING

◄ Ask the children to imagine this scene: It's Halloween night and they're in a haunted house. The house is very dark, there are cobwebs everywhere, and the floorboards are creaking.

◄ Now ask the following questions:
- How does your face look?
- How do your hands show that you're afraid?
- How do you walk? Run?
- If you were standing still and trying to hide in a corner, how would your body look?

AFTER

◄ Ask the children what they might do to stop being scared. Encourage them to demonstrate.

Show Me What You're Feeling

BEFORE

◄ Discuss with the children all the feelings included in this activity (see below), particularly those they've yet to experience through movement.

◄ Discuss the fact that there are really only two ways to express emotions: with words and with the body.

DURING

◄ Explain to the children that you're going to express or create an emotion with words (or verbally). They will demonstrate through their facial expressions and body positions how your words make them feel. (Remember that the way you use your voice will be very important in conveying the appropriate emotion.)

◄ You might include the following:
- What a surprise!
- Ouch!
- Goody, goody!
- Oh no—what am I going to do?
- Yucky!
- I don't have anyone to play with.
- I'm so proud of myself!
- Boo!
- I love you!

ALSO

◄ Try the same activity later, but this time the children will be moving. Ask them to begin walking around the room.

◄ Present one of the verbal expressions from the above list, and encourage the children to respond by moving (or simply walking) in the way the words make them feel.

◄ Allow enough time for them to express the emotion before presenting the next one.

◄ Vary the length of time between presenting emotions so the children don't know when to expect the next one.

AFTER
• **Feelings** *by Aliki or* **The Feelings Book** *by Todd Parr*

◄ Read and discuss Aliki's *Feelings* or *The Feelings Book* by Todd Parr.

Feeling Calm/Feeling Nervous

BEFORE

◄ Naturally, you can only expect the children to respond to those emotions with which they've had experience. For example, it's unlikely they would be able to depict such "adult" emotions as *disillusionment* or *anxiety*. However, *calm* and *nervous,* although more of a challenge than the emotions in previous activities, are feelings the children can relate to if you spend some time discussing them.

◄ Explain that calm is a very relaxed feeling, such as the way they feel just before falling asleep at night. At those times, muscles feel loose and "liquid." Images that can help describe relaxation include feeling like a rag doll, a limp noodle, or a wet washcloth. Other times when children might have experienced calmness include while sitting by a lake, observing a bird soar through the sky, or watching the sun set.

◄ What are some times when the children have felt nervous? Explain that being nervous is sort of a combination of being scared and worried. Have they ever:
  • worried that it might rain on the day of a big outing?
  • lost sight of their parents in a big store and felt scared until spotting them again?

◄ How did their muscles and bodies feel at those times? Were they loose or tense? Ask them to show you.

DURING

◄ The children are going to experience the differences between feeling calm and feeling nervous at various levels in space. Begin the activity with the children standing.

◄ When you say the word "calm," the children should make their bodies as relaxed as possible.

◄ When you say "nervous," they tense up. (Vary the time between verbal cues. Also, remember that the quality of your voice is very important; it should sound like the word you're saying.)

◄ Repeat the process with the children kneeling, sitting, and, finally, lying down.

ALSO

◄ This is an excellent relaxation technique to use any time the children need to unwind a bit. Creating "calmness" in the body is a learned skill and a wonderful tool in controlling stress.

◄ In fact, there are those who believe that controlling tension can help children learn better.

AFTER
- *Paint, paintbrushes, and paper*
- *Two pieces of music (one soft and the other fast and frenzied)*

◁ Provide the children with paint, paintbrushes, and paper. Then play a piece of slow, soft music.

◁ After a while, change the music to a piece that's fast and frenzied.

◁ How does the children's artwork change?

◁ To regain a sense of calm, end with the slow music!

Health Awareness

In the Beginning

Learning Objectives
• *To acquaint the children with the five basic food groups*
• *To encourage the children to eat well*

BEFORE

◄ Where does bread come from? Why, the supermarket, of course! (Although some "enlightened" children might say the bakery.)

◄ However, back in the "olden days," children knew where bread really came from—it was made in their homes from flour and water and yeast, and it filled the house with a wonderful aroma.

◄ Talk to the children about this basic food, explaining that it doesn't originate on the grocer's shelves.

◄ Describe the process of mixing flour and water and yeast into dough, kneading it, letting it rise, rolling it out with a rolling pin, shaping it to fit a bread pan, and baking it.

DURING

◄ Explain to the children that you're going to be the baker and they're going to be the ingredients. And when you're through with them, they're going to be loaves of bread, all ready to eat!

◄ Use the appropriate hand and arm movements for each step of the following process, pretending to do each step to the children.

◄ They, in turn, will pretend to have the following *done* to them. The process is as follows:

◄ Stir the flour and water and yeast together (the children are the flour, water, and yeast).
- Knead the dough.
- Cover the dough with a cloth and let it rise.
- Punch down the dough.
- Roll out the dough.
- Shape the dough into a loaf.
- Let the dough rise again.
- Bake the dough (it rises even more and becomes firm).
- Remove the bread from the pan.

ALSO

◄ Ask the children to take on the shapes of other types of dough, including the following:
- A pretzel
- A muffin
- A gingerbread man
- A round loaf

AFTER

- **Bread, Bread, Bread** *by Ann Morris*
- *Ingredients and equipment for making bread*

◄ For a social studies connection, take the children on a field trip to a bakery where they can see breadmaking in action!

◄ Or, for a hands-on math experience, bake bread with the children in the classroom.

◄ Read *Bread, Bread, Bread* by Ann Morris, which includes photos by Ken Heyman of breads from around the world, to add language arts, art, and social studies.

From Cow to Cone

BEFORE

◄ Dairy products are an important food group. They are a good source of calcium, which helps keep our bones and teeth strong. The most common dairy product for most children is milk, but their favorite is probably ice cream.

◄ Although the process described in the song below is not strictly correct, it will give the children an idea of the process involved in creating ice cream from milk and of the relationship among several dairy products.

◄ Talk to the children about the process. Explain that after the cow is milked, the cream rises to the top and is skimmed off.

◄ The cream is churned into butter, which can then be made into ice cream by stirring it as it freezes. (Ice cream is most often made from cream, but can also be made from butterfat.)

DURING

◄ Sing the following song to the tune of "The Farmer in the Dell." With the children, decide which movements go with the verses (I've included some possibilities) and sing it with the children:

From Cow to Cone
The farmer milks the cow. (make a milking action with hands and arms)
The farmer milks the cow.
Hi-ho the dairy-o,
The farmer milks the cow.

Second verse
The farmer skims the cream… **(make a skimming motion, as though using a ladle)**

Third verse
The farmer churns the cream… **(do an up-and-down motion with one hand above the other, as though holding a broom handle)**

Fourth verse
The farmer stirs the butter… **(make a stirring motion)**

Fifth verse
The butter turns to ice cream… **(pretend to lick ice cream in a cone)**

Sixth verse
The ice cream slowly melts… **(pretend to be melting ice cream)**

AFTER

◄ Visit a dairy farm if there is one nearby. Otherwise, a trip to the local ice cream shop will do!

BEFORE
• Pictures of vegetables, optional

◁ Vegetables are not known to be the favorite food group of most children. In fact, a cajoling, "Eat your vegetables" is probably the most common line spoken to children at the dinner table!

◁ This activity may help give the children an awareness of some vegetables' origins and an appreciation for the work that goes into preparing them.

◁ Talk to the children about the vegetables and the following actions.

◁ Show the children pictures of vegetables, if you have them.

DURING
◁ Ask the children to pretend to do the following:
- Pull a carrot out of the ground
- Put a carrot into the blender (to make carrot juice)
- Wash lettuce
- Pull apart lettuce leaves
- Peel an onion
- Chop an onion
- Peel potatoes
- Mash potatoes

ALSO
◁ Challenge the children by giving them an opportunity to pretend to *be* the vegetables. Ask them to pretend to be the following:
- A carrot being pulled out of the ground
- A carrot in the blender
- Lettuce being washed
- Lettuce being pulled apart
- An onion being peeled
- An onion being chopped
- A potato being peeled
- A potato being mashed

AFTER
• Ingredients for a salad, salad dressing, plates, and forks

◁ Make a big salad (one that includes lettuce, carrots, and onions) with the children. They may be more inclined to eat salad once they have an appreciation for some of the veggies that go into it!

Fruit, Glorious Fruit

BEFORE
* *Pictures of fruit, optional*

◂ Fruit is one of the five basic food groups (the others are bread products, dairy products, vegetables, and proteins). Fruits provide us with lots of vitamins and minerals and are fun to eat.

◂ But fruit is also special because you can make so many things to eat and drink with the many varieties.

◂ What are the favorite fruits of the children in your group? Can they name some of the foods and drinks that are made with them?

◂ If possible, show the children pictures of different fruits. Also, discuss the relationship between grapes and raisins.

DURING

◂ The children can either pretend to *be* or *do* the following activities and items, depending upon their interpretations. For example, some might show you what it's like to pour the orange juice, while others show you what it's like to be the orange juice being poured.

◂ The important thing is that the children consider the multiple possibilities for a single fruit.

◂ Ask the children to show you the following:

* *Oranges*
  An orange being peeled
  An orange section
  Orange sherbet being scooped
  Orange juice being poured

* *Apples*
  An apple hanging from a tree
  An apple slice
  An apple pie
  Applesauce simmering on the stove

* *Bananas*
  A banana being peeled
  A loaf of banana bread
  A banana muffin
  A banana slice floating in cereal and milk

* *Grapes*
  A bunch of grapes hanging on a vine
  Grape jelly being spread
  A raisin
  A slice of raisin toast

AFTER
◂ Take a field trip to the grocery store to look at and discuss the wide variety of fruits. You could also buy some to make a fruit salad!

A Balanced Diet

BEFORE
• *Construction paper or poster board and markers*

◄ Review the four food groups explored in the previous activities, and introduce the fifth group—proteins. The protein group includes fish and meats, as well as products that belong in other food groups (for example, beans and cheese).

◄ To have a healthy, balanced diet, people should eat a certain amount of food from each of the five basic groups each day.

◄ On a piece of construction paper or poster board, make lists of foods and drinks that fall under each of the food group categories. Or cut out pictures from magazines and paste them under the headings.

DURING
◄ Divide the children into groups of five and instruct them to create, with their bodies, a well-balanced meal.

◄ This involves deciding who is to belong to which food group, and then specifically which foods and drinks to be.

◄ Whatever foods and drinks the children choose, they should be recognizable. In other words, each child should find a way to look or move so that his choice can be guessed with a minimum of effort.

◄ Give the children enough time to work this out.

◄ You can either move from group to group, acting as the guesser, or you can ask one group at a time to demonstrate while the rest of the class guesses.

ALSO
◄ If the class isn't large enough to divide into groups of five, write each food group on a scrap of paper and put them into a hat or bag. Assign each child to a food group by asking him to select a scrap of paper from the bag.

◄ You then act as "chef," creating one meal at a time by asking for a vegetable, a fruit, a dairy product, a bread product, and a protein.

◄ One child from each of these groups comes to the center of the room (the "plate") and poses or moves like the food or drink of his choice.

◄ Then, the guessing takes place.

AFTER
• **Eating (Small World)** *by Gwenyth Swain*

◄ Read and discuss *Eating (Small World)* by Gwenyth Swain.

Washing Hands

Learning Objectives
- *To call attention to the importance of good hygiene*
- *To make hygiene seem like fun, so the subject will have a pleasant association*

BEFORE

◄ One of the most important aspects of good hygiene is handwashing. Children need to learn early that washing their hands with soap and warm water eliminates germs and can help prevent colds and other illnesses from being spread.

◄ Germs, however, are a puzzling concept to young children. After all, they have no evidence that germs really exist!

◄ Talk to the children about germs, explaining that some of the ways they're spread are through touching, sneezing, and coughing.

◄ That's why it's important when you have a cold to wash your hands following each sneeze or cough.

DURING

◄ Ask the children to stand in a circle and hold hands.

◄ Explain that they're going to move around in a circle while you chant the following rhyme.

◄ Every time they hear the word *achoo,* they should stop, let go of each other's hands, and pretend to wash their hands in the center of the circle (the "sink").

◄ Then they re-join hands and continue to walk around in a circle as you chant again. The chant is as follows:

> *I am a germ;*
> *I can be spread*
> *From you to you to you.*
> *All it takes is a cough or a sneeze—*
> *I'll get you with an "achoo!"*

ALSO

◄ Once the children have the hang of this, vary the tempo at which you recite the chant, saying it slowly, quickly, and at a moderate tempo.

AFTER

• **Those Mean Nasty Dirty Downright Disgusting but...Invisible Germs *by Judith Anne Rice***

◄ Read and discuss *Those Mean Nasty Dirty Downright Disgusting but...Invisible Germs,* written by Judith Anne Rice. (It's available in both English and Spanish.)

BEFORE

◄ Chances are, the children in your class are not yet taking care of their own hair. So pretending to do so in the following activity should make them feel more "grown-up."

◄ Talk to them about all the things necessary to have clean, attractive-looking hair, stressing the fact that hair care is also a part of good hygiene.

DURING

◄ The following song is performed to the tune of "Here We Go 'Round the Mulberry Bush."

◄ Familiarize the children with it so they can sing it with you as they act out the words.

◄ On the last verse, the children can pretend to admire themselves in a mirror.

Hair Care

This is the way we wash our hair,
Wash our hair, wash our hair.
This is the way we wash our hair
So early in the morning.

(Second verse)
…rinse our hair…

(Third verse)
…towel it dry…

(Fourth verse)
…blow it dry…

(Fifth verse)
…comb our hair…

(Sixth verse)
…look so nice…

AFTER

• **Those Itsy-Bitsy Teeny-Tiny Not-So-Nice Head Lice** *by Judith Anne Rice*

◄ Talk about the diverse possibilities for hair color and styles. How many children have brown, blonde, or black hair? How many different shades of each are there? How many have curly or straight hair? Long or short?

◄ Read and discuss *Those Itsy-Bitsy Teeny-Tiny Not-So-Nice Head Lice* by Judith Anne Rice.

Rub-a-Dub-Dub

BEFORE

◀ Talk to the children about bathing. Ask them:
- What do you like best about it?
- Does the water feel good?
- Do you like the slipperiness of the soap?
- Does scrubbing with a washcloth make your skin feel tingly?

DURING

◀ In addition to being an exercise in hygiene, the following poem is great for body parts identification.

◀ Encourage the children to act out the lines accordingly, pretending to wash the body parts mentioned.

Rub-a-Dub-Dub

Rub-a-dub-dub
I sit in my tub,
Washing my face and ears.
My face will shine.
It'll look so fine,
And I'll be able to hear!

Rub-a-dub-dub
I sit in my tub,
Washing my hands and arms.
They'll be so clean.
They'll practically gleam,
And I will feel like a charm!

Rub-a-dub-dub
I sit in my tub,
Washing my back and tummy.
My body will glow
From head to toe,
And I am going to look yummy!

Rub-a-dub-dub
I sit in my tub
Washing my legs and feet.
I'll make them shine,
Because they're mine.
Being clean is such a treat!

AFTER
• Washcloths, towels, combs, brushes, and dolls

◀ Put washcloths, towels, combs, brushes, and dolls in the Housekeeping Area so the children can practice good hygiene as "parents."

BEFORE

◀ Talk to the children about the importance of brushing their teeth. Discuss problems such as tooth decay and gum disease.

◀ Ask them:
- How many times a day do you brush your teeth?
- What kind of toothpaste do you use?
- What color toothbrush do you have?

DURING

◀ The children are going to pretend to be various things involved with brushing teeth. Ask them them to think carefully about each of the following actions before demonstrating what they look like.

◀ Encourage the children to pretend to be these items:
- A tube of toothpaste
- A tube of toothpaste being rolled up from the bottom
- A tube of toothpaste that's been squished all over
- Toothpaste being squeezed from the tube
- The shape of a toothbrush
- A toothbrush in motion
- A battery-powered toothbrush

AFTER
• *"Brush Your Teeth" by Raffi*

◀ Play Raffi's "Brush Your Teeth" from his *Singable Songs for the Very Young*.

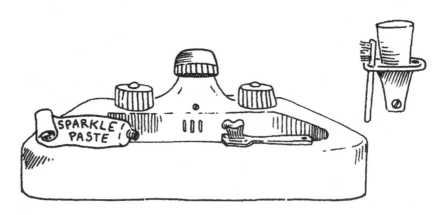

Caring for Our Clothes

BEFORE

◁ Clean clothes are almost as important as a clean body on which to put them.

◁ Ask the children, "What are some of the ways we can take care of our clothes?

◁ Possible responses include washing, ironing, folding, and hanging them properly.

DURING

◁ Ask the children to pretend to do the following:
  - Put clothes into the washing machine
  - Wash and wring clothes by hand
  - Hang clothes on a clothesline
  - Iron
  - Put clothes on hangers
  - Fold clothes and place them in a drawer

ALSO

◁ For a greater challenge, ask the children to choose an item of clothing they'd like to be (for example, a pair of pants, a shirt, and a skirt).

◁ Then encourage them to take on the shape of that piece of clothing and show you what it would look like when the following things are being done to it:
  - Washed in a washing machine
  - Washed and wrung by hand
  - Tumble-dried
  - Dried on a clothesline in the breeze
  - Ironed
  - Hung on a hanger
  - Folded and placed in a drawer

AFTER
  - *Items of clothing, hangers, clothesline, and clothespins*

◁ Place various items of clothing, hangers, a clothesline, and clothespins in the Housekeeping Area. If you've got washbasins and empty laundry detergent containers, add them for even more fun!

Follow the Leader

Learning Objectives
- To enhance body and spatial awareness
- To strengthen imaginations
- To practice locomotor and nonlocomotor skills

BEFORE

◄ This activity serves three purposes:
- It provides practice with various locomotor and nonlocomotor skills;
- It offers an opportunity for the children to physically imitate what they're seeing; and
- It serves as an exploration of various movement elements.

◄ *Locomotor* movement transports the body from one place to another while *nonlocomotor* movement occurs as the body remains in place.

◄ Before you begin, explain to the children that you are going to lead them around the room as you move in a variety of ways. Explain that they should try to look and move as much like you as possible.

DURING

◄ Lead the children around the room, performing any locomotor skills that they know how to do (for example, walking, jogging, jumping, and galloping). Pause occasionally to perform a nonlocomotor skill, such as shaking, bending, stretching, or twisting.

◄ Be sure to alter the force (heavy/light) and time (slow/fast) of your movements and to incorporate a variety of body shapes. (Possible shapes include large, small, wide, narrow, and crooked.)

ALSO

◄ When the children are ready, ask them to be the leaders.

AFTER
- *Manipulatives, optional*

◄ Discuss the meaning of such terms as *lead, follow, in front of, behind,* and *in the middle.*
◄ Ask the children, "When would you use these words?"
◄ Invite the children to demonstrate with manipulatives.

How Many Parts?

BEFORE

◄ Nonlocomotor movements are performed with the body remaining in one spot. While people can do all of these movements with the whole body, there are also a number of body parts that can execute these skills.
◄ Explain this to the children, perhaps choosing one nonlocomotor skill from the following list and demonstrating it.

DURING

◄ First, ask the children to show you how the whole body performs each skill on the list.

◄ Then, ask them to find out how many body parts can also perform them.

◄ Allow enough time for the children to experiment with each skill.

◄ Nonlocomotor skills can include:
  • Shaking
  • Bending
  • Stretching
  • Twisting
  • Swinging

ALSO

◄ Once the children have had ample experience with nonlocomotor skills, challenge them to play the Mirror Game (page 17) with partners.

◄ Facing each other, one partner begins by making some simple movements that his partner must "reflect."

◄ After a while, partners switch roles.

AFTER

◄ Many nonlocomotor skills involve the body's joints. Use this opportunity for a discussion of such joints as elbows, knuckles, wrists, knees, and ankles.

◄ If possible, show the children a diagram of a skeleton of the human body!

BEFORE

◄ Explain to the children that they're going to go on an imaginary walking trip through many different environments.

◄ Then, talk specifically about what it would be like to walk through the various environments mentioned in the following poem.

◄ Also, discuss any terms that may require explanation, such as *briskly* and *waning*.

DURING

◄ Read the following poem as the children pretend to walk as described.

> **A Walking Trip**
> *Briskly we start out*
> *On a bright sunny day;*
> *We have lots of energy*
> *To get us on our way!*
>
> *Up a steep, steep hill,*
> *Then down the other side,*
> *Once again on flatter ground*
> *We can lengthen our stride.*

We pause at the curb
Looking left, looking right,
Waiting 'til it's safe to cross
Between the lines of white.

Now through a meadow
With grass so tall and green,
And across the slippery rocks
Of a swift shallow stream.

Into the forest,
It's almost dark as night,
With thousands of leaves above
Keeping out the light.

Tangles of branches,
Fallen trunks, roots, and rocks
Make this the most challenging
Of places for a walk.

Our energy is waning,
The pace begins to slow,
Can it be that we still have
The return trip to go?!

ALSO

◄ If time allows, try reversing the order of the environments, asking the children to continue with the return trip.

◄ You won't be able to do it in rhyme, but making the return trip provides an opportunity for repetition with some variety.

AFTER

◄ Walking is a simple, everyday activity we can do to get and stay fit. Talk to the children about making physical activity as much a daily habit as brushing teeth.

◄ Then go out and take a real walk with them!

Getting Nowhere

BEFORE

◄ Talk to the children about the difference between locomotor and nonlocomotor movement (locomotor movement transports the body from one place to another; nonlocomotor movement occurs while the body remains in place).

◄ Explain, however, that a number of locomotor movements, such as walking and running, can be performed in place. And that's what they're going to experiment with in this activity.

◀ Make sure to challenge the children with only those skills with which they've had success.

DURING
◀ Ask the children to perform the following locomotor movements *in place*.
  - Walking
  - Running
  - Jumping
  - Hopping
  - Galloping
  - Skipping

ALSO
◀ To add interest to the activity, include one of the variations below to each of the above skills. Then every time you repeat this activity, you can mix and match the variations and skills differently.
  - Very quickly
  - In slow motion
  - As though on hot sand
  - Lightly
  - Strongly
  - In a happy-go-lucky way

AFTER
- **Anna Banana: 101 Jump-Rope Rhymes** *by Joanna Cole*

◀ Explain to the children that there are few times in life when we'd actually gallop or skip in place. But what are some times when we might jump or run in place?
◀ This would also be a great time to introduce the children to jump rope rhymes. You can find plenty of them in *Anna Banana: 101 Jump-Rope Rhymes* by Joanna Cole.

BEFORE
- *Paper and marker*
- *Container*

◀ Talk to the children about the parades they've seen. Ask them:
  - What was in the parade you saw?
  - Were there animals? What kinds?
  - What musical instruments did you see and hear?
◀ Discuss all of the possibilities mentioned below.
◀ Write the names of various people and things found in parades on scraps of paper. Then, place them in a container.

DURING

◁ Write a component of a parade on separate scraps of paper and put them into a bag. Ask each child to draw a piece of paper.

◁ Then encourage them to form a "parade," depicting whatever person or thing they've chosen.

◁ Possibilities include:

- Drummers (bass and snare)
- Flutists
- Trumpeters
- Trombonists
- Cymbal players
- Saxophonists
- Horses
- Fire engines
- Flag bearers
- Banner carriers (must be an even number)
- Baton twirlers
- Floats

ALSO

• *Marching music*

◁ To add an extra element to this activity, accompany it with a piece of marching music. John Philip Sousa has written some great ones, but you'll also find marches on Hap Palmer's *Mod Marches*.

AFTER

◁ What are some holidays or celebrations in this country and others when parades are held? Use this opportunity to discuss one or more of them with the children.

Seasons

Autumn Leaves

Learning Objectives
• *To foster greater appreciation for all autumn has to offer*
• *To develop a better understanding of the transition from summer to winter*

BEFORE

◄ The changing colors of the leaves and their inevitable fall from the trees are what many people think of first when they think of autumn.

◄ Talk to the children in basic terms about what happens to the leaves. Explain that the cool nights cause the leaves to change from green to bright orange, yellow, gold, or red, and how the autumn winds eventually blow them from their branches. (This will require additional explanation if the children don't live in a climate where this phenomenon occurs.)

DURING

◄ Explain to the children that they are going to pretend to be autumn leaves:

• First, they are green and hanging on branches.

• Then, the weather gets cooler and the leaves change colors. (The children will each have an interesting interpretation for this challenge!)

• Suddenly, the wind begins to blow (you can pretend to be the wind, if desired).

• The leaves are separated from their branches and begin to fall to the ground—but then another gust of wind sends them twirling in the air.

• After a while, the wind stops and the leaves land on the ground.

• Finally, someone (you!) comes along and rakes all the leaves into a great big pile!

AFTER

• *Fallen leaves, paper, markers, crayons, glue, and tape*
• **Autumn by Gerda Muller**

◄ If you have colorful autumn leaves on the ground where you live, bring the children outside to gather some. Then, encourage them to create works of art with them. If you don't live in an area with fallen leaves, make some leaves using appropriately colored construction paper with the children.

◄ Put Gerda Muller's *Autumn,* a wordless board book, in the Reading Area.

Picking Apples

BEFORE

◄ Autumn is apple-picking time in many parts of the country. Tell the children that apples are grown in orchards and explain the process of picking apples. (If they've never been to an orchard, they may think apples come from supermarkets!) Talk about the feel, smell, and taste of this freshly picked fruit.

DURING

◄ The children are now ready to act out the following poem.

◄ Read it as slowly as you need to, and encourage them to portray the actions realistically.

Picking Apples

Just out of reach,
So high in the tree
Is a juicy red apple
Waiting for me.

Get on my toes
And stretch up my hand,
But I can't reach no matter
How tall I stand.

So I must jump
As high as I can,
'Til I have that apple in
My little hand!

I make it shine;
My job is complete.
My juicy red apple is
Ready to eat!

AFTER
• **Variety of apples**

◄ If you have an apple orchard nearby, take the children for an apple-picking visit! If not, bring in a variety of apples from the grocery store and discuss their origins, as well as their similarities and differences.

The School Year Begins

BEFORE

◄ In many areas of North America, the month of September brings both the beginning of autumn and the start of the school year. Talk to the children about the first day of school.

◄ Discuss all the things parents and children do to prepare for the school year, such as buying pencils and paper, a lunch box, and new clothes.

◄ What else comes to the children's minds when they think about beginning a school year?

DURING

◄ This is a *being* and *doing* activity, which means the children alternate between pretending to be something and pretending to do something. Ask them to show you the following:

- **Being**
  A pencil
  A lunchbox
  A sweater
  A chalkboard
  A ruler

- **Doing**
  Sharpening a pencil
  Making a sandwich
  Putting on a sweater
  Writing on a chalkboard
  Measuring something

AFTER

◄ Show and Tell is a great activity to help children get to know one another at the beginning of the school year.

◄ Ask the children to bring in something they got for the new school year, or something that reminds them of school.

Squirrels

BEFORE
- *Pictures of squirrels, optional*

◀ Talk to the children about squirrels. What do they look like? How do they move? Ask the children:
  - What do squirrels eat?
  - How do they look when they're eating?

◀ Explain that during autumn, many animals (including squirrels) begin collecting and storing food (mostly nuts) for the winter so they'll have enough to eat until spring.

◀ If there are a lot of squirrels in your area, try and bring the children outdoors for a squirrel sighting! If not, show the children pictures if you have them.

DURING
◀ Ask the children to show you how a squirrel would do the following:
  - Swish its tail
  - Climb a tree
  - Eat food from between its paws
  - Leap from one tree to another
  - Hold nuts in its mouth
  - Bring food to a nest in a tree

AFTER
- **A Pack of Ragamuffins (*a Grimm's fairy tale), any version**

◀ Read *A Pack of Ragamuffins,* a Grimm's fairy tale in which a hen and a rooster set out to gather nuts before the squirrel gets them.

◀ Also, if you haven't done so already, go outside for that squirrel sighting!

The Nature of Autumn

BEFORE

◄ When we think of autumn and nature, there are several things that come to mind—cooler temperatures, windy days, falling leaves, pumpkins, and so on.

◄ What do the children think of? What do they like best about autumn?

DURING

◄ Ask the children to show you how they would move if they were:
  • The wind
  • Falling leaves
  • Feeling chilly
  • Raking leaves
  • Trying to walk against the wind
  • Playing in the leaves
  • Picking up and carrying a huge pumpkin

AFTER

• *Outdoor thermometer, optional*
• **Pumpkin Pumpkin** *by Jeanne Titherington*

◄ If you live in an area with fallen leaves, bring the children outside to rake them and play in them. It's great exercise and great fun!

◄ How about a field trip to a pumpkin patch?

◄ If neither of these ideas is possible, hang an outdoor thermometer outside a window and ask the children to record the daily temperature. Does the temperature drop as autumn progresses?

◄ Read Jeanne Titherington's *Pumpkin Pumpkin* to the children.

Winter Sports

Learning Objectives
• *To foster greater appreciation for all winter has to offer, both indoors and out*
• *To encourage the children to consider the nature of winter*

BEFORE
• *Pictures depicting winter activities*

◄ Winter in cold climates lends itself to a number of outdoor activities. Three of the most popular cold weather outdoor activities are skiing, skating, and sledding. Talk to the children about the differences among these activities, especially emphasizing the movements that each requires.

◄ Show the children pictures of the three different activities. (For children living in areas where these activities are not common, pictures are especially helpful.)

DURING
◄ Teach the children the following song, sung to the tune of "Farmer in the Dell."

◄ Encourage them to act out the sport mentioned in each verse. (Leave enough time between verses so they can adequately portray each sport.)

Winter Sports
Sledding down the hill,
Sledding down the hill,
Hi-ho away I go,
I'm sledding down the hill!

(Second verse)
Skiing down the hill…

(Third verse)
Skating 'cross the ice…

ALSO
• *Waltz music and paper plates*

◄ Play a recording of a waltz (Emil Waldteufel's *Skater's Waltz* and Johann Strauss's *Skater's Waltz* are perfect) and ask the children to imagine that they're figure skating in the Olympics.

◄ Such skating involves grace and elegance, as well as skillfully executed jumps and turns.

◄ If you simply want them to experience the gliding motion of skating, provide each child with a pair of paper plates to use as ice skates!

AFTER
• *Art materials, such as paper, markers, glue, and glitter*

◄ If possible, bring the children outside to participate in something "wintery."

◄ Provide a variety of art materials and encourage them to create sleds, skis, or winter scenes.

BEFORE
• *Pictures of animals that hibernate, optional*

◄ Because the normal food supply of certain birds and animals is not always available during winter months, these creatures must hibernate. What they're actually doing is lowering their normal body temperatures in order to save energy, but children usually think of animals' hibernation as "going to sleep" for the winter.

◄ Talk to the children about hibernation and some of the animals that practice it. For example, bears often hibernate in caves, while groundhogs hibernate under the ground, burrowing through tunnels to reach their nests. If possible, show the children pictures of these animals.

ACTIVITY

◄ Ask some of the children to form "tunnels" that lead underground.

◄ The remaining children act as groundhogs, making their way from the surface of the ground, through the tunnels, and to their nests.

◄ When the groundhogs reach their nests, they curl up and go to sleep. (If time permits, repeat this activity and ask the children to reverse roles.)

ALSO

◄ Divide the children into groups of three.

◄ Ask two of the children to form a cave, while the third pretends to be a bear.

◄ With the onset of winter, the bear makes its way into the cave and falls asleep. (If possible, repeat the activity so that each child gets a chance to be a bear.)

AFTER
• *Homemade or purchased tunnel or sheet*

◄ Set up a homemade or purchased tunnel in the classroom to offer the children an opportunity to practice cross-lateral movement (for example, crawling and creeping). This type of movement is very important in getting both sides of the brain to "talk" to one another.

◄ Or, hang a sheet in a corner, forming a "cave" for quiet times.

Baby, It's Cold Outside!

BEFORE
• *Bowls of cold and warm water, optional*

◄ Asking the children to experience (or imagine) opposites, in alternation, is a wonderful way to make a point. In this exercise, the children are going to consider the cold by comparing it with its opposite—heat.

◄ Talk to the children about hot and cold. Ask them:
  • What things are the coldest? The hottest?
  • How do cold and hot make them feel?
  • How do their bodies react to each?

◄ Put out bowls of cold and warm (not hot!) water and encourage the children to dip their fingers into them.

DURING
◄ Explain to the children they're going to really have to use their imaginations for this activity.

◄ Encourage the children to show you how their bodies would move or look if they were:
  • Outside in the freezing cold
  • Soaking in a hot tub
  • Outdoors in the winter without mittens
  • Warming their hands by a fireplace
  • Drinking ice water on a winter day
  • Drinking hot cocoa on a winter day
  • Rubbing their faces with snow
  • Pressing a wet, hot washcloth to their cheeks
  • Making angels in the snow without a jacket
  • Snuggling in a nice, warm bed

AFTER
• **Winter** *by Gerda Muller*

◄ Place Gerda Muller's *Winter,* a wordless board book, in the Reading Area.

BEFORE

• *Pictures of snow or snow scenes, optional*

◁ Children love snow and all that it has to offer. Even children who've never experienced snow are fascinated by the idea of it.

◁ Ask the children:

- What do you like best about snow?
- Have you ever built a snowperson?
- How did you do it?
- What did it look like when it was all done?
- What happens to a snowperson when the days are sunny and the weather gets a little warmer?

◁ Talk about snowflakes and how no two are alike.

◁ Discuss what happens to a snowball when it's rolled downhill and gathers more snow.

◁ Pictures of snow are especially helpful for children living in warmer climates.

DURING

◁ Encourage the children to pretend to be snow in a variety of forms. Ask them to show you how they would look if they were the following:

- A snowflake falling
- A snowball that starts small and gets bigger as it rolls down a hill
- A snowperson being built (from beginning to end)
- A snowperson melting

AFTER

◁ The last two images, used one after the other, make a wonderful relaxation exercise! Simply stress to the children that becoming a snowperson and melting are *slow* processes.

◁ You might also want to follow this activity with a rousing rendition of "Frosty the Snowman!"

The Fireplace

BEFORE

◄ Keeping warm is a major part of winter, and many people keep their homes warm with fireplaces.

◄ Ask the children how many of them have fireplaces or wood stoves at home.

◄ Talk to them about the work involved in chopping and stacking wood and in building a fire.

◄ Ask the children:
- What does fire look like?
- How does it move?

DURING

◄ With the children, sing the following song to the tune of "London Bridge." Encourage them to act it out as they sing. (The fourth verse can include crumpling newspaper, laying the wood, and striking the match.)

The Fireplace

This is how I chop the wood,
Chop the wood, chop the wood.
This is how I chop the wood
On this wintry day.

(Second verse)
…stack the wood…

(Third verse)
…carry the wood…

(Fourth verse)
…build a fire…

ALSO

◄ Ask the children to act like pieces of wood, and arrange them in an imaginary fireplace. The "kindling" can be lying on the floor, with the rest of the "wood" arranged at various levels around the kindling (kneeling, squatting, standing bent over, and standing straight).

◄ Pretend to light a match at the kindling level. The children, one level at a time, begin to move like "dancing" flames. (Although pieces of wood are usually piled on top of each other, you will want to arrange the children so they're near each other but not quite touching. Or, emphasize the importance of the "pieces of wood" leaning gently against one another.)

AFTER

• *Blocks, Legos, or other manipulatives*

◄ Encourage the children to construct their own fireplaces using blocks, Legos, or other manipulatives.

Learning Objectives
• *To foster appreciation for all spring has to offer*
• *To develop a better understanding of the transition from winter to summer*

BEFORE

◄ Explain to the children that seeds lie dormant in the ground throughout the winter.
◄ In spring, with the return of warm temperatures and the help of both the rain and the sun ("April showers bring May flowers"), seeds slowly begin to grow into flowers. First, they poke up through the ground and then gradually blossom into their full glory.

DURING

◄ Teach the children the following song, sung to the tune of "The Itsy Bitsy Spider."
◄ After you've sung it together, ask them to imagine that they're tiny seeds in the ground. Encourage them to lie on the floor and make themselves into the smallest shapes possible.
◄ Move throughout the room, pretending to be the rain falling on each of the seeds.
◄ Next, act like the sun and "shine" on the seeds, warming them up.
◄ The seeds begin to grow—very slowly—eventually poking through the ground and blossoming into the most beautiful flowers on earth!

Seeds

The itsy bitsy seed
Lies deep within the ground.
First comes the rain;
Feel it falling down.
Then out comes the sun
And dries up all the rain,
And the itsy bitsy seed
Can start to grow again.

AFTER

• *Seeds, potting soil, paper cups*
• *The Tiny Seed by Eric Carle*

◄ With the children, plant seeds in paper cups and place them on a windowsill.
◄ Water the seeds and watch for daily progress.
◄ Read Eric Carle's *The Tiny Seed* to the children.

Melting Snowpeople

BEFORE

◄ If you live in a cold weather climate, ask the children:
  • Did you build a snowperson during the past winter?
  • What did it look like?
  • Was it large or small?

- If you live in an area without snow, simply talk about snowpeople. Ask the children:
  - What shape are most snowpeople?
  - What happens to the snowpeople when spring comes and it gets warmer?

DURING
- Ask the children to each pretend to be a snowperson—just like one they might have built. Can they make themselves as round as possible?
- Once they've assumed the shapes they want, you can pretend to be the shining sun.
- Ask the children to imagine that their snow is getting warmer and warmer, until it finally begins to melt.
- The snowpeople continue melting—very slowly—until they're nothing but puddles on the ground.

ALSO
- You can do this activity immediately after Seeds (page 58) as a study in contrast, or you can use it as a relaxation exercise.

AFTER
- *Water, freezer, and paper cups*

- Freeze water in paper cups.
- Put them on a windowsill in the sunlight.
- Help the children time how long it takes for the ice to melt.

Butterflies

BEFORE
- *Pictures of the stages of the life cycle of a butterfly, optional*

- *Metamorphosis* is the word used to describe the life cycle of a butterfly. There are four stages: egg, caterpillar, chrysalis, and butterfly
- The egg is very tiny and is usually laid under the leaf of a plant.
- The caterpillar is long and tubular in shape, and it has six eyes on each side and several pairs of legs.
- The chrysalis hangs from a tree by a silken thread and represents the "resting" stage; the butterfly begins to form inside the chrysalis.
- Finally, an adult butterfly emerges from the chrysalis. It has bright, colorful wings that are exactly the same on both sides. While resting, the butterfly holds its wings vertically, almost touching each other over the back of the body.
- If possible, show the children pictures of caterpillars and a variety of butterflies.

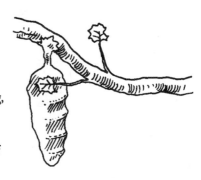

DURING

◄ Explain to the children that they are going to act out the life cycle of a butterfly, beginning with the egg.

◄ Ask them to make themselves as small as they can and pretend to be a tiny egg underneath a leaf. (If desired, ask half of the children to act like eggs, while the others kneel over them to represent leaves.)

◄ The "eggs" then turn into long and tubular caterpillars. Ask them to show you how caterpillars move. Can several of the children join together to form one long caterpillar?

◄ Next, the children experience the motionlessness of being a chrysalis, either by lying on the floor or by pretending to hang from the branch of a tree from a silken thread. (Some children could portray trees and others the thread.)

◄ Finally, the children move like butterflies. They can pretend to fly, drink nectar from flowers, or rest.

AFTER

• **Insects and Squiggly Things** *by Jane Murphy*

◄ Choose songs from Jane Murphy's *Insects, Bugs and Squiggly Things.*

Free at Last!

BEFORE

◄ Talk with the children about how it feels to be all bundled up in winter clothes. What kinds of clothes must they wear in winter (sweaters, heavy jackets, snowsuits, scarves, mittens, hats, heavy socks, boots, earmuffs, and so on)?

◄ Now, ask them how spring makes them feel. Do they enjoy shedding all those extra clothes?

DURING

• *Light and airy music, such as Bach's* **Anna Magdalena Notebook,** *optional*

◄ As an option, you can choose a piece of music that's light and airy to accompany this activity. Pieces from Bach's *Anna Magdalena Notebook* are great to use.

◄ Ask the children to pretend to be dressed in the winter items you previously discussed. Are they warm? Do they feel like they weigh a lot more than usual?

◄ Now ask them to show you what it would look like to remove those items, one by one. Do they feel cooler? More free?

◄ Once the children are "unencumbered," ask them to show you how that freedom makes them feel like moving. Does it make them feel like dancing or skipping? (For children who are developmentally ready, this can be a good opportunity to introduce or practice the latter skill.)

AFTER

- **Art materials, such as paper, markers, scissors, and glue**
- **Dolls, and winter and spring doll clothing**

◄ Ask the children to draw someone dressed first in winter clothing, and then in spring clothes.

◄ Or, place dolls and both winter and spring clothing in the Housekeeping Area.

Spring Cleaning

BEFORE

◄ Spring is a time for renewal. Flowers and leaves return, as well as the birds that flew south for the winter. Windows are opened to the fresh spring air after months of being closed. The warmth and sunshine make people feel renewed and more energetic. Often people use this extra energy to renew their surroundings as well by making their homes fresh and like new. This is called spring cleaning!

◄ What household chores might family members have to do when spring cleaning? Possible responses include washing windows or floors, painting walls, shaking out carpets, putting up new curtains, vacuuming, and putting away winter clothes.

DURING

◄ Sing the following verses to the tune of "Whistle While You Work" as the children act out the movements involved. (Sing the song slowly, and leave plenty of time between verses!)

Spring Cleaning

Smiling while you work
To make the windows shine.
Around and 'round
And 'round and 'round
To make them look so fine!

Smiling while you work,
You're vacuuming the rug.
Go back and forth
And back and forth,
Yes, you deserve a hug!

Smiling while you work
To give the walls fresh paint.
Go up and down
And up and down
To make the house look quaint!

Smiling while you work,
New curtains look so nice.
We stretch and bend
And stretch and bend
To make home paradise!

AFTER
- ***Child-size brooms, dust cloths, and paintbrushes***
- ***Paintbrushes and buckets of water***

◀ Place brooms, dust cloths, and paintbrushes in the Housekeeping Area so the children can get their fill of spring cleaning!

◀ You can also bring the children outside and give them paintbrushes and buckets of water. Encourage them to "paint" the outside of the building! The children will get some much needed exercise, and they'll also learn lessons about wet and dry, light and dark, and evaporation.

Water Sports

Learning Objectives
• To foster greater appreciation for all summer has to offer
• To encourage the children to consider the nature of summer

BEFORE

◄ Summer is the time for water sports!

◄ Talk to the children about the sports listed below. Ask them if they've ever performed or watched any of them.

◄ Ask them what movements are involved in each sport. (If desired, show the children pictures of the sports to help them envision them.)

DURING

◄ Ask the children to show you the movements involved in performing the following sports (give the children ample time to explore each one):
  • Swimming
  • Water skiing
  • Rowing a boat
  • Paddling a canoe
  • Surfing
  • Fishing

AFTER

◄ Sing "Row, Row, Row Your Boat" with the children.

◄ Then, ask them for other ideas (for example, "Paddle, Paddle, Paddle Your Canoe").

The Nature of Summer

BEFORE

◄ When we think of nature and summer, many images come to mind. Ask the children what they picture when they think of summer and nature.

◄ Be sure to include a discussion of the images listed below. If possible, show them pictures of those things with which the children are less familiar.

DURING

◄ Ask the children to show you, with their bodies, what they think the following things look like:
  • The shining sun
  • A flower
  • A bumblebee
  • A tomato hanging on a vine
  • Gentle rain
  • Cornstalks rustling in the breeze
  • A fluffy white cloud
  • Grass
  • The heat

AFTER
- **Summer** *by Gerda Muller*

◀ If you're in session during the summer, bring the children outdoors and encourage them to find one item that really "says" summer to them.

◀ Place Gerda Muller's *Summer,* a wordless board book, in the Reading Area.

The Thunderstorm

BEFORE

◀ For some children, thunderstorms are a scary aspect of nature that occur during the summer. However, by talking about them with the children (and encouraging them to explore thunderstorms through movement), you can help alleviate their fears while broadening their knowledge.

◀ Explain that thunder and lightning are simply the result of hot and cold air meeting in the sky. Ask the children to describe thunder, lightning, storm clouds, heavy rain, and wind. What are the colors of storm clouds and lightning? What are their shapes? What are the sounds of rain, wind, and thunder?

DURING

◀ Ask the children to move as they imagine the following elements of a storm do. (Their individual interpretations should be interesting!)
- Dark clouds
- Heavy rain
- Wind
- Lightning
- Thunder

ALSO

◀ Ask the children to imagine that they're dark clouds. The "clouds" begin to come together, a few at a time, in the center of the room (like storm clouds gathering).

◀ Then, when all of the clouds are together, a thunderstorm develops.

◀ Ask the children to move, as a group, like a thunderstorm.

AFTER
- *Art materials, such as paper, markers, glue, and glitter*

◀ Provide a wide variety of art materials and encourage the children to create a picture of what a thunderstorm looks like.

The Picnic

BEFORE

◄ Picnics are a popular activity during the summer. Ask the children:

- Have you ever been on a picnic?
- Can you describe a picnic?
- Where were the picnics held?
- What did you eat?
- Did you have a picnic basket and a blanket?
- What do you like best about picnics?

DURING

◄ Children love stories, and they love to imagine themselves in them.

◄ Tell the children the following brief story, and ask them to act it out as you read.

One warm sunny day, the children of the [name of your school or center] decided to go on a picnic. So they made some sandwiches and packed them in picnic baskets. Then they set off for the park. It felt so good to be outdoors! The sun was shining, and the air smelled so fresh. When the children arrived at the park, they chose the perfect spot on the grass, beneath the low-hanging branches of a willow tree, to spread their blanket. Then they all sat down on the blanket, opened up their picnic baskets, and ate the food they'd packed. When they were finished, the children picked up their napkins and scraps of food and threw them in the trash barrel. But then they were tired. So they went back to the blanket, and they laid down and fell asleep under the willow tree!

AFTER

◄ Have a picnic—indoors or out!

The Barbecue

BEFORE

◄ Many people cook a lot of their meals in the summer by barbecuing. Discuss barbecuing with the children. Talk about the shapes and sizes of barbecue grills, the way charcoal looks (before and after it's lit), and the process involved in barbecuing.

◄ Be sure to specifically discuss the images listed below.

DURING

◄ Encourage the children to pretend to be a number of things related to barbecues. Ask them to show you the following:

- The shape of a barbecue grill
- Lighter fluid being squirted from a container
- A match being struck and lit
- Coals heating up
- Something sizzling on the grill

AFTER

- **Eating** *by Gwenyth Swain*

◄ Read Gwenyth Swain's *Eating* to the children to stimulate a discussion of the kinds of foods people enjoy in different places.

Holidays and Celebrations

Halloween Shapes

Learning Objectives
• *To stimulate the imagination*
• *To foster an appreciation for the fun aspects of Halloween*

BEFORE
• *Pictures of Halloween images (such as a witch's hat and a bat), optional*

◄ Halloween, with its many images, provides a great opportunity to explore the movement element of shapes. Ask the children what they think of when they hear the word *Halloween,* and then use their responses, as well as the images listed below, as part of your activity.

◄ If possible, show the children pictures of Halloween images, such as a witch's hat, a bat, and a skeleton.

DURING

◄ Ask the children to show you, with their bodies, the shapes of Halloween. Possibilities include:
- A witch's hat
- A pumpkin
- A broom
- A trick-or-treat bag
- A candle and flame
- A cupcake
- A bat (the flying kind)
- A cat
- A skeleton
- A ghost
- A candy bar

AFTER
• *Ingredients for baking Halloween cupcakes, or*
• *A pumpkin and carving knife (teacher only)*

◄ Bake Halloween cupcakes or carve a pumpkin with the children!

If I Could Be...

BEFORE

◄ Children love to pretend, and they almost always have a favorite person, character, or thing they like to pretend to be (although it can change from day to day!).

◄ Explain to the children that they're going to pretend it's Halloween night and that they can be anything they want.

◄ Give them a few moments to decide what they'd most like to be.

DURING

◄ Ask the children, one a time, what person or thing they most want to be on Halloween.

◄ After the child has told you, ask him to show you how that person or thing moves.

◄ If time permits, ask the rest of the class (as a whole) to show you their interpretations of each child's fantasy.

AFTER
• *Art materials, such as paper, markers, glue, and glitter*

◄ Provide a wide variety of art materials and encourage the children to draw a picture of what they plan to be on Halloween.

The Wicked Witch

BEFORE

◄ As everyone who has seen *The Wizard of Oz* knows, there are good witches and bad witches. Ask the children:
   • What did the wicked witches in *The Wizard of Oz* and *Snow White* look like?
   • What did they wear?
   • How did they sound?

◄ Discuss that in stories, bad witches ride broomsticks and mix up "potions" in cauldrons. Be sure to mention such physical characteristics as gnarled hands and hunched backs.

DURING

◄ The children are going to act out the creation of a potion, or witch's brew, from the conception of the idea to the finished product.

◄ Ask the children to pretend to be a wicked witch doing the following:
   • Wringing her hands as she plans her potion
   • Measuring ingredients into the cauldron
   • Stirring the brew
   • Tasting the brew (it's going to be hot!)
   • Adding more ingredients
   • Stirring and tasting again
   • Measuring the brew into a vial (or small container)
   • Flying off on her broom

AFTER
• *Large pots and spoons, brooms*

◄ Put large pots, spoons, and brooms in the Dramatic Play Center so the children can further pursue their "witch" pretend play.

Halloween Means. . .

BEFORE

◄ Halloween means different things to different children. Some children are excited by the prospect of a school party, others look forward to dressing up and pretending to be something or someone else, and some think only of the candy they're going to get. Others are frightened by the idea of goblins, skeletons, and so on.

◄ Talk to the children about what Halloween means to them. What do they like most about Halloween? What do they like least? Why?

DURING

◄ Ask the children to show you the following:
  • Being excited
  • Feeling scared
  • Walking as though scared
  • Putting on their costumes
  • Admiring their costumes in the mirror
  • Eating something yummy
  • Eating something yucky
  • Having a tummy ache after eating too much candy
  • Sharing their candy with friends

AFTER

◄ What are other times when food is a big part of a celebration? Encourage the children to describe how their families partake in some of these occasions.

Black and Orange

BEFORE

◄ Black and orange are the traditional colors of Halloween. Discuss this with the children and show them examples of both black and orange.

◄ Ask them what comes to mind for each of these colors. Black is the darkest color there is, and orange is a very bright color. How does each color make them feel?

DURING

◄ Ask the children to show you how the color black makes them feel like moving. How does the color orange make them feel like moving? How does Halloween make them feel like moving?

◄ Then, read the following poem and ask them to move in the ways they described.

> **Black and Orange**
>
> Black is oh so very dark—
> The opposite of light.
> Black cats, black hats, black sky above,
> The color of the night!
>
> Orange is so very bright—
> Just like the shining sun.
> Orange fruit and orange drinks,
> A color meant for fun!
>
> But put them both together,
> And black and orange mean
> The spookiest of holidays,
> The fun of Halloween!

AFTER
• *Black and orange art materials, markers, scissors, and glue*

◄ Give the children a variety of black and orange art materials and encourage them to create a Halloween picture.

The Meal: Before and After

BEFORE

‹ The Thanksgiving Day dinner is a tradition as old as the holiday itself. And even though sharing the feast with family and friends is something to be eagerly anticipated, it requires a great deal of work (as do most worthwhile projects), both before and after.

‹ Discuss this with the children. Ask them to tell you some of the chores that must be done before and after the meal.

DURING

‹ Ask the children to show you how they would move to perform these tasks:
  • Rolling pie dough
  • Peeling and slicing apples
  • Stuffing the turkey
  • Basting the turkey
  • Peeling potatoes
  • Mashing potatoes
  • Setting the table
  • Serving the meal
  • Clearing the table
  • Washing dishes

AFTER

‹ Practice real-life table setting with the children.

Counting Blessings

BEFORE

◄ Explain to the children that the purpose of Thanksgiving is to take some time to consider our blessings and feel appreciation for all we have. These blessings may include family, friends, pets, good health, food to eat, a home, and so on.

DURING

◄ Ask each child, in turn, what he is most grateful for or what his favorite thing is.

◄ Then, ask him to show you that blessing through movement.

ALSO

◄ If time permits, ask the rest of the class (as a whole) to show you their interpretations of each child's blessing.

AFTER

◄ As a follow-up, plan a session of Show and Tell and ask the children to bring in one of their favorite things (or people!).

Pilgrims and American Indians

BEFORE

◄ Discuss the historical origins of Thanksgiving with the children. Explain that the pilgrims came to America and found the first winter to be very difficult. However, the Native Americans taught them many things about finding and growing food, which enabled them to survive

◄ The first Thanksgiving in this country was a meal shared by the American Indians and the pilgrims.

DURING

◄ Divide the children into two equal groups of "pilgrims" and "Indians."

◄ Ask the pilgrims to stand side-by-side, facing the Indians, who are also standing side-by-side. (There should be a pilgrim opposite every Indian, a few feet apart.)

◄ Encourage the Indians to act out the following things, as though instructing the pilgrims.

◄ Each pilgrim should imitate the movements of the Indian who is opposite him.

◄ Possible actions can include:

- Fishing
- Picking cranberries
- Shucking corn
- Shooting a bow and arrow
- Picking corn
- Chopping wood

◄ When all of the actions have been done, the pilgrims and Indians come forward to shake each other's hands.

ALSO
◄ If time permits, ask the children to change roles so that everyone has a chance to "lead" and a chance to imitate. Or, the next time you perform this activity, make sure that the children play the opposite role.

AFTER
- **One Little, Two Little, Three Little Pilgrims** *by B. G. Hennessy*
- **Squanto and the Miracle of Thanksgiving** *by Eric Metaxas*
- **Three Little Pilgrims** *by Janet Craig*

◄ Read *One Little, Two Little, Three Little Pilgrims* by B. G. Hennessy, *Squanto and the Miracle of Thanksgiving* by Eric Metaxas, or *Three Little Pilgrims* by Janet Craig to the children.

The Food: Before and After

BEFORE
◄ Unless a child has had experience with the preparation of food, he is likely to think that *cooked* is the food's natural state and it simply arrives in that state to the dinner table! Talk to the children about all the foods listed below, discussing where they come from and the differences between their natural and cooked states.

DURING
◄ Ask the children to show you, with their bodies, the way the following foods look in both their "before" and "after" states. Possibilities include:
- A cranberry and cranberry sauce
- A potato and mashed potatoes
- A carrot and a cooked carrot slice
- An apple and applesauce
- A pumpkin and a pumpkin pie
- A squash and cooked squash

AFTER
- *Ingredients and cooking materials for making applesauce*

◄ Make applesauce with the children. It's easy enough to do and since most children are familiar with applesauce only from a jar, it will be a new experience for them. It will also be a lesson in mathematics and science.

Thanksgiving Things

BEFORE

◄ Explain to the children that they are going to pretend to be a number of inanimate objects associated with Thanksgiving.

◄ What makes the activity especially challenging is that these inanimate objects are having something done to them.

◄ Talk in detail about the following actions. Feel free to add any others that you or the children might think of.

DURING

◄ Ask the children to show you how it would look if they were the following:

- An ear of corn being shucked
- Potatoes being mashed
- Pie crust being rolled
- A dish being washed
- An apple being sliced
- A salad being tossed
- A candle melting

AFTER

• *Art materials, such as paper, markers, scissors, and glue*

◄ Provide a variety of art materials and encourage the children to create a picture of the thing that most reminds them of Thanksgiving.

◄ Ask family members to visit the classroom to share stories of how they celebrate Thanksgiving.

The Menorah

Learning Objectives

• For Jewish children, these activities provide opportunities to experience and appreciate Hanukkah in a new way

• For non-Jewish children, the activities help them to become more familiar with the holiday and gain an appreciation for traditions other than their own

BEFORE

• **Menorah or picture of one, optional**

◄ Hanukkah, also known as the Festival of Lights, is an eight-day celebration. One of the symbols of the holiday is the menorah, which is a candleholder with nine candles. The *shāmmāsh* is the center candle, and it's used to light each of the other eight candles—one for each night of the celebration.

◄ Explain this to the children and, if possible, show them a menorah or a picture of one.

DURING

◄ Ask the children to hold their thumbs together, side-by-side, and make fists with their remaining fingers. Their thumbs will symbolize the *shāmmāsh* and their fingers the other eight candles.

◄ As you begin to count from one to eight (slowly at first), the children lift their fingers, one at a time, to symbolize the lighting of the candles.

◄ They can then "extinguish" each candle by folding their eight fingers back toward their palms as you count backward from eight to one.

ALSO

◄ Repeat this activity several times, varying the tempo of your counting.

AFTER

• **Art materials, such as paper, markers, scissors, and glue**

◄ Provide a variety of art materials and encourage the children to create their own menorahs.

Eight Candles for Eight Nights

BEFORE

◄ This is another counting activity that will help the children to remember the eight candles for the eight nights of Hanukkah. Before starting, remind them of the eight-day celebration and the menorah.

DURING

◄ Sing the following song to the tune of "Ten Little Indians." Sing slowly to allow the children to pretend to light (counting aloud as they do) the right number of candles. For example, if you've just sung "five," they pretend to light five candles as they count from one to five.

◀ The song is as follows:

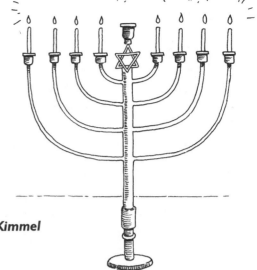

Eight Candles for Eight Nights
One little, two little, three little candles
Four little, five little, six little candles,
Seven and eight little candles,
One for every night!

AFTER
- **Hershel and the Hanukkah Goblins** *by Eric A. Kimmel*
- **The Story of Hanukkah** *by Norma Simon*

◀ Read *Hershel and the Hanukkah Goblins,* written by Eric A. Kimmel and illustrated by Trina Schart Hyman or *The Story of Hanukkah* by Norma Simon.

The Candle

BEFORE
◀ As the children are by now aware, the candle is an important symbol of Hanukkah. Talk to the children about candles, such as their shapes, what they're made of, how their flames move, and how they melt.

DURING
◀ Ask the children to each assume the shape of a candle (keeping in mind that children may have seen candles in a variety of shapes).
◀ Then move around the room and "light" each candle individually. (How can the children show they've just been lit?
◀ The children pretend to burn for a while before they begin melting.
◀ Encourage them to continue melting until the wax is just a puddle.

ALSO
◀ You can use this as a relaxation exercise any time the children need to unwind a bit.

AFTER
- *Empty toilet paper tubes and art materials*

◀ Give each child an empty toilet paper tube, which will serve as a candle, and a variety of art materials with which to decorate it.

A Festival of Lights

BEFORE

◄ Because Hanukkah is the Festival of Lights, talk to the children about the shining of lights (including candles and stars, which are associated with this holiday). How does the light, as opposed to the dark, make them feel?

DURING

◄ Ask the children to close and open their eyes a few times as one way of experiencing dark versus light. (Vary the length of time they keep their eyes closed.)

◄ Then explain that, for this activity, *closed* means dark and *open* means light, and ask how else they can show light and dark with their bodies.

◄ Possibilities include opening and closing the following:

- Mouth
- Hands
- Arms
- Legs
- Knees
- Feet
- The body as a whole

AFTER

◄ Invite the parents of Jewish children, or someone from the community, to come in and talk about how their family celebrates this holiday.

Star of David

BEFORE

• *Picture of the Star of David, optional*

◄ Show the children a picture of the Star of David or draw one for them (two triangles intersecting to create a six-pointed star). Explain that this, too, is a Jewish symbol.

◄ Discuss the shape of the star with the children.

DURING

◄ Ask the children to each show you, with their bodies, the shape of the Star of David.

◄ Can they show you how it would look if the star were shining brightly?

ALSO

◄ Challenge the children to pair off and create the shape with a partner.

AFTER

• *Art materials, such as paper, markers, scissors, and glue*

◄ Give the children a variety of art materials and encourage them to create their own stars.

Christmas Shapes

Learning Objectives
• *To strengthen appreciation for the spirit of giving*
• *To help the children more fully experience the joy that is part of this holiday*

BEFORE

◄ Children can never have too much experience with the movement elements of shape and space. Christmas, with its many images, certainly lends itself to the exploration of these elements.

◄ Talk to the children about the shapes of the images below. (Feel free to add to the list!)

DURING

◄ Ask the children to show you, with their bodies, the shape of the following:
  - A Christmas tree
  - An ornament
  - A snowperson
  - A bell
  - A chimney
  - A star
  - A reindeer
  - A Christmas present
  - The bow on top of a present
  - Tinsel
  - A wreath
  - A sled

AFTER

◄ Invite some parents to come in and talk about their holiday traditions.

Stringing Popcorn

BEFORE

◄ In these modern times, many children may never have strung popcorn for a Christmas tree. In fact, they may never have even seen such a thing.

◄ Describe this special decoration to them, beginning with the popping of the corn and ending with hanging the string on the tree. (Or bring in a string of popcorn to show them.)

◄ Explain that one wraps the string of popcorn around the tree in "tiers," just like garland or a string of lights.

DURING

◄ Explain to the children that you're going to make a string of popcorn—with them as the popcorn! Ask them to get into the smallest shape possible, each pretending to be a kernel of corn.

◄ Then move around the room and "turn on the heat" under all of the kernels, which begin to "pop."

◁ When the "popcorn" is fully cooked, link the pieces together, one at a time, by pretending to run a needle and thread from the fingertips of one child's hand to the next. (In other words, the children join hands.)

◁ Finally, when the string is complete, the children circle an imaginary tree (or a real one, if possible) and sing the following song to the tune of "Here We Go 'Round the Mulberry Bush."

Stringing Popcorn

Here we go 'round the Christmas tree,
The Christmas tree, the Christmas tree.
Here we go 'round the Christmas tree,
So early Christmas morning.

ALSO

◁ After the "popcorn" has been strung, ask the children to see how many shapes the string can assume. They can try this as a circle (with all of their hands linked) and as a line (with two of the children letting go).

AFTER

- *Ingredients and equipment for making popcorn*
- *Plastic sewing needles and thread*

◁ Make popcorn with the children. Then, use plastic sewing needles and thread to make popcorn strings. Decorate the room with them!

Being Santa

BEFORE

◁ Santa Claus is one of the things children love most about Christmas. In this activity, they are going to have a chance to "be" him.

◁ Talk to the children about Santa. Ask them:
- What does Santa look like?
- What does he wear?
- What do you like best about him?

DURING

◁ Ask the children to show you how Santa might do the following things. (Remind them that their portrayals should be as realistic as possible.)
- Walk
- Drive his sleigh
- Walk along a rooftop
- Come down a chimney
- Carry his bundle of presents
- Arrange his presents around a tree
- Hand out presents to children
- Laugh!

AFTER
• *Art materials, such as paper, markers, scissors, and glue*

◁ Children love to draw Santa Claus. Give them a variety of art materials and encourage them to create their own version of this character.

A Christmas Dance

BEFORE
• *Recording of Christmas music*
• *Pictures of Christmas characters, optional*

◁ Choose a recording of Christmas music (preferably one that is both lively and familiar to the children).

◁ This activity is based on the game of Statues, which requires the children to move while there is music playing and to freeze into "statues" when the music stops. It's a wonderful activity because it offers the children an opportunity to express themselves through "improvisation." And because they think of it as a game rather than as dance improvisation, they are not self-conscious about doing it. Therefore, the children might feel more comfortable with the idea of playing Statues (using Christmas characters) than with doing a Christmas dance.

◁ Talk about the characters that the children will be portraying and discuss how each might move. Show them pictures, if possible.

DURING
◁ Play the music you've chosen, stopping and starting it at random intervals (lift the needle if it's a record, or press the pause button for a tape or CD).

◁ Each time you stop the music, ask the children to become (and move like) a new Christmas character. Characters can include the following:
  • Santa Claus
  • A reindeer (Rudolph perhaps)
  • An angel
  • One of Santa's elves
  • Frosty the Snowman

AFTER
• *Book with the story of "Frosty the Snowman" or "Rudolph," any version*

◁ Read the story of "Frosty the Snowman" or "Rudolph" to the children. Place the books in the Reading Center so the children can return to them again and again.

The Spirit of Giving

BEFORE

◄ Christmas is a time for giving, which is something that children who anxiously look forward to receiving can easily overlook.

◄ You can help to emphasize the giving aspect by talking about it with the children. Ask them:
  • Do you have any plans for gift giving this holiday season?
  • What are you giving and to whom?
  • If you could give one person absolutely anything in the whole world, what would you give and to whom? Why?

DURING

◄ Ask the children to stand in a circle, and explain that you're going to ask them to move in certain ways.

◄ However, instead of doing movements all together, the children will do them in turns. In other words, one child performs a movement, then "gives" it to the child beside him. This continues all the way around the circle, which each child repeating it.

◄ Offer the suggestions below, all with Christmas in mind. However, each leading child can perform the movement any way he chooses.

◄ Begin each round of movement with a different child.

◄ Possible suggestions include:
  • A handshake
  • Christmas lights blinking
  • A reindeer shaking its head
  • A bell ringing
  • Chopping down a Christmas tree
  • Waking up Christmas morning
  • A smile!

AFTER

◄ Bring the children to a local nursing home, where they can offer the residents some holiday cheer!

Kwanzaa Candles

BEFORE
• *Picture of a kinara, optional*

◄ Kwanzaa is an African-American celebration of the oneness and goodness of life. As it is in so many other celebrations, the candle is an important symbol of Kwanzaa. The kinara is a candleholder that represents the stalk, from which all life springs. It holds seven candles, called the mishumaa (mee-SHOO-mah), which represent the Seven Principles of Kwanzaa.

◄ Explain, as simply as possible, that the kinara is a candleholder that represents life and the seven candles it holds stand for seven important things about the celebration of Kwanzaa.

◄ • Show the children a real kinara or a picture of one, if possible.

DURING

◄ Ask the children to show you the shape of the following:
  • A candleholder
  • A candle
  • A flame
  • The number seven
  • The letter "K"

◄ Now encourage them to move as though they were:
  • A flickering flame
  • A drop of wax sliding down the side of a candle
  • A puddle of wax that's still liquid
  • A puddle of wax that's cooling and hardening

ALSO

◄ If you can arrange the children into groups of eight, you can challenge them to take on the roles of the kinara and its seven candles. One child will take on the shape of a candleholder, with the remaining seven children taking on the shape of the candles in front of the "kinara."

◄ As you count from one to seven, each child demonstrates its candle being "lit."

AFTER
• **Seven Candles for Kwanzaa** *by Andrea David Pinkney and/or* **K Is for Kwanzaa: A Kwanzaa Alphabet Book** *by Juwanda G. Ford*

◄ Read *Seven Candles for Kwanzaa* by Andrea David Pinkney and/or *K Is for Kwanzaa: A Kwanzaa Alphabet Book* by Juwanda G. Ford.

Learning Objectives
• *For those children whose families celebrate Kwanzaa, these activities provide opportunities to experience and appreciate the festivities in a new way*
• *For those children unfamiliar with the celebration, the activities offer an introduction to Kwanzaa and an appreciation for traditions other than their own*

CHAPTER FOUR • Holidays & Celebrations

More Kwanzaa Symbols

BEFORE

◄ In addition to the kinara and the mishumaa, there are five other primary symbols of Kwanzaa. They are:

- Mkeka (M-kay-cah): the straw mat symbolizing tradition;
- Muhindi (Moo-heen-dee): the ear of corn representing the offspring, or children, in the family;
- Kikombe cha umoja (Kee-coam-bay-oo-moe-jah): the Unity Cup, symbolizing the first principle of Kwanzaa, which is the unity of family, community, nation, and race;
- Zawadi (Sah-wah-dee): the gifts representing the fruits of the labor of the parents and the rewards of the seeds sown by the children; and
- Karamu: the feast that brings the community together to exchange and give thanks.

◄ Explain these meanings to the children, as simply as you can. If possible, show them pictures of these symbols.

DURING

◄ Ask the children to show you movements that represent the following:

- A straw mat
- An ear of corn
- A cup
- Pouring something from the cup
- Drinking something from the cup
- Receiving a gift
- Giving a gift
- Eating a feast

AFTER

- **Together for Kwanzaa by Juwanda G. Ford**

◄ Read *Together for Kwanzaa* by Juwanda G. Ford. You might also bring in, or ask the children to bring in, Kwanzaa symbols.

Who Am I?

BEFORE

◄ The second principle of Kwanzaa is kujichagulia (koo-jee-cha-goo-LEE-ah), or self-determination. It refers to defining, naming, creating for, and speaking for oneself.

◄ Explain to the children, as simply as possible, that self-determination means being an individual, the best one can be. What do each of the children like best about themselves?

DURING

◄ Ask the children to stand in a circle.

◄ Then, one at a time, each child moves to the center of the circle, states his name, and physically demonstrates one of his favorites thing to do.

◄ Following each demonstration, all of the children imitate the movement involved. For example, Kayla goes into the center of the circle and says, "My name is Kayla." She then depicts swimming or ice-skating, for example. The rest of the children then do the same.

AFTER

• *Art materials, such as paper, markers, scissors, and glue*

◄ Encourage each child to create a self-portrait.

Past, Present, and Future

BEFORE

◄ A major concept of Kwanzaa is helping Black Americans relate to the past in order to understand the present and deal with the future. Talk with the children about ways in which this might be possible. For example, if we make a mistake in the past, it affects us in the present, but we don't have to make the same mistake again in the future.

DURING

◄ Ask the children to stand side-by-side at one end of the room.

◄ Tell them that when you say the word *future*, they're to take a step forward. When you say *past*, they should take a step backward. And when you say *present*, they should walk in place.

◄ Then play the game, varying the order in which you present the words and sometimes repeating the same one!

ALSO

◄ Once the children are familiar with this game, substitute other locomotor skills, such as jumping or hopping.

AFTER

◄ Invite adult members of families who celebrate Kwanzaa to visit the classroom and share stories of why and how they celebrate.

We Are Community!

BEFORE

◄ The concept of community plays an enormous role in Kwanzaa. In fact, the sixth principle, kuumba (koo-OOM-bah), stands for creativity in doing as much as possible to leave the community more beautiful and beneficial than when it was inherited.

◄ Talk to the children about the idea of community. What does it mean to them and their families? What do they think could be done to make their community better?

DURING

◄ Teach the children the following song, sung to the tune of "We Are Family."

We Are Community

We are community.
I've got all my friends here with me.
We are community
Being the best that we can be.
We are community.
We'll change the world; wait and see!
We are community! [Big finish!]

◄ Now ask the children to stand with you in a circle, holding hands.

◄ As you sing the song together, raise your arms and move toward the center of the circle every time you sing, "We are community."

◄ Move back out during the pause between lines. On every other line, walk rhythmically around in a circle.

ALSO

◄ When the children are ready, challenge them to create new movements to accompany the lines of the song.

AFTER

◄ Encourage the children to choose a project to benefit the community. Possibilities include collecting canned goods, outgrown clothes, or toys for less fortunate families.

◄ Or, perhaps they could clean up an area in need of "sprucing."

Happy New Year!

BEFORE
• *Noisemaker, confetti, and a party hat*

◄ Bring in a noisemaker, some confetti, and a party hat.

◄ Discuss the meaning of this holiday with the children. Explain that this holiday gives people a whole new year to look forward to! It's fun and exciting to think of all the things you want to do in the coming year, so people celebrate the arrival of this holiday in a lot of different ways.

◄ Some of the images that come to mind when we think of New Year's Eve and New Year's Day are listed below. Talk about them with the children (their meanings as well as their physical characteristics).

DURING

◄ Ask the children to pretend to be the following:
- A noisemaker
- Confetti that has been tossed
- The ball in Times Square
- A clock
- A party hat on someone's head
- A calendar with its pages being turned

AFTER
• *Art materials, such as paper, markers, scissors, and glue*

◄ Ask the children to create their own calendars with the art materials.

The Clock

BEFORE
• *Clock*

◄ Explain to the children that on New Year's Eve, most adults stay up late. They look forward to the stroke of midnight, which is the signal that the New Year has officially begun. Therefore, a clock is an important part of the New Year celebration.

◄ Using a clock or a clock face, show the children what 12:00 and 6:00 look like.

DURING

◄ You are going to be the clock in this activity. Raise your right arm over your head to the 12:00 position and put your left arm down, center front.

◄ Then bring your right arm sideways and down in a smooth arc to center front, where it meets your left arm. When your palms touch, it's 6:00.

◄ Then, separate both arms and sweep them out and up. When they meet overhead at 12:00, the children stop their movement.

The children, meanwhile, begin moving (in any way they want) when the "clock" begins moving, and they stop when the clock strikes 12.

They should match their tempo to the speed of the clock's movements.

When the clock strikes six, they'll know the time for moving is half over.

ALSO

Each time you perform this activity, vary the speed of the clock's hands.

AFTER

• *Art materials, such as paper, markers, scissors, and glue*

Provide a variety of art materials and encourage the children to create their own clocks.

Number One Day

BEFORE

• *Index cards or pieces of paper with a 0, 1, 2, 3, 5, or 6 written on each one*

Explain to the children that there are 365 days in a year, and that January 1st is the first day of the first month. That's why it's called New Year's Day!

This activity will give the children a chance to explore the element of shape, while giving some thought to numbers.

Post the numbers 0, 1, 2, 3, 5, and 6 someplace that is visible to all the children.

DURING

Ask the children to show you the number 1 with their bodies. How many parts of their bodies can they use to make the number 1 (for example, a finger, an arm, a leg, a foot, and a toe)?

Explain that there are 12 months in a year. Ask them to make a number 1 with their bodies, followed by a number 2.

Now explain that there are 365 days in a year. Ask the children to make a number 3, 6, and 5.

After New Year's Day, there are 30 days left in January. Can they make a number 3, followed by a zero?

ALSO
• Masking tape or rope

◁ When the children are developmentally ready, challenge them to make some of these numbers with partners.

◁ Or, create some of these numbers on the floor with masking tape or rope. Challenge the children to move along the pathways using a variety of locomotor skills, such as walking, hopping, and galloping.

AFTER
• Felt or other material and scissors

◁ Cut out numbers from felt or other material. Place them someplace where the children can have access to them, making it possible for them to continue exploring these concepts.

The Countdown

BEFORE

◁ Again, explain the importance of midnight on New Year's Eve. Help the children understand the anticipation leading up to midnight.

◁ Talk to them about the countdown that takes place during the ten seconds before midnight. Ask them if they have ever heard a countdown, perhaps just before a space shuttle was launched.

◁ Tell them that at the end of the countdown, at the stroke of midnight, people shout "Happy New Year!" and cheer, making a lot of noise.

DURING

◁ Ask the children to freeze into a "statue," get into a small shape on the floor, or stand with their hands over their eyes as you count backward from 10.

◁ When you get to "zero," they shout, "Happy New Year," jump up and down, and make noise. Begin the countdown again, after they have resumed their original positions.

◁ Repeat often, each time counting down at a different tempo.

ALSO
• Noisemakers, musical instruments, or pots and pans and wooden spoons

◁ If you really want to let the children get some noise out of their systems, provide party noisemakers, musical instruments, or pots and pans and wooden spoons!

AFTER
• Rhythm band instruments

◁ Give the children rhythm band instruments and invite them to hold a New Year's parade.

Resolutions

BEFORE

◀ Keep in mind that it can't be easy for a young child to understand all the talk about New Year's resolutions. However, you can help by explaining that January 1st marks the beginning of a new year. Therefore, people like to "begin again" by making promises to do or improve some things in the coming year. For example, a person might make a promise (a resolution) to do something he hasn't gotten around to in the past year, such as cleaning out the garage or painting the house.

DURING

◀ Ask each child, in turn, what he might resolve to do in the New Year and to act it out for you.

ALSO

◀ If time permits, ask the rest of the class (as a whole) to show you their interpretations of each child's resolution.

AFTER

• *Art materials, such as paper, markers, scissors, and glue*

◀ Give the children writing or art materials so they can write or draw their resolutions.

Feelings

BEFORE

◄ Explain to the children that the reason for Valentine's Day is so people can demonstrate that they care for one another. However, it's okay (actually, it's great!) to show caring feelings all the time. In fact, it's a good idea to express all of our emotions and to communicate all of our feelings.

◄ Ask the children:
  • What are some of the feelings you experience?
  • What makes you feel that way?
  • How do you show those feelings?

DURING

◄ Ask the children to show you how the following emotions make their bodies look or move:
  • Happiness
  • Surprise
  • Sadness
  • Anger
  • Fear
  • Pride
  • Confusion
  • Love!

AFTER
• **Feelings *by Aliki* or I Was So Mad! *by Norma Simon***

◄ Read, or reread, Aliki's *Feelings* or Norma Simon's *I Was So Mad!*

Learning Objectives
• *To foster understanding of the reason for this holiday*
• *To encourage the expression of feelings*

Playing Cupid

BEFORE
• *Picture of Cupid, optional*

◄ Explain to the children that Cupid is a fictional character who supposedly helps people fall in love by shooting them with his magical bow and arrows. He is red, looks like an angel (or cherub), has wings, and flies. This can't be easy for the children to imagine, so it would be helpful if you show them a picture.

◄ Discuss Cupid's characteristics and role as thoroughly as possible.

DURING

◄ Ask each child to imagine that he is Cupid. Encourage them to show you how Cupid would do the following things. (The last suggestion is wide open for individual interpretation. It will be interesting to see what they come up with!)

- Fly
- Deliver Valentines
- Shoot his magical arrows
- Deliver flowers to people
- Make people fall in love

AFTER
- *Art materials, such as paper, markers, scissors, and glue*

◁ Provide a variety of art materials and ask the children to create a picture of Cupid. (Be sure they know you don't expect them to model it after the picture you showed them.)

Sending Cards

BEFORE
◁ One of the most popular ways for people to show their affection on Valentine's Day is by sending cards. Who would the children like to send cards to?

DURING
◁ Explain to the children that they are going to act out the process of sending Valentine's Day cards, from choosing them to mailing them.
◁ Ask them to pretend to do the following:
- Buy a card at a store
- Sign the card
- Put it in an envelope
- Seal the envelope
- Address the envelope
- Stamp the envelope
- Mail the card

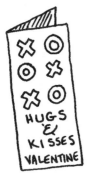

ALSO
◁ Ask the children to pretend that they are the cards.
- What shape do they want to be?
- Can they show you how they open and close?
- Can they pretend to slip into and out of an envelope?
- Can they pretend to go through the slot in the mailbox and then slide down?

AFTER
- *Art materials, such as paper, markers, scissors, and glue*

◁ Give the children an opportunity to make their own Valentine's Day cards.

I Can Show I Care

BEFORE

◄ Again, Valentine's Day is specifically meant for showing others that we love and care for them. Who do the children care for? How do they show it?

DURING

◄ The following poem gives the children a chance to depict a variety of ways to display caring feelings.

◄ Although the poem refers to "I" and "you," each child should act out the poem as an individual, relating to an imaginary partner.

I Can Show I Care

I can show I care by
Reaching out my hand,
By giving you a gentle touch
To say I understand.

I can show I care by
Giving you a smile,
To make you feel like smiling, too,
For just a little while.

I can show I care by
Giving you a hug–
Wrap my arms around you 'til
You feel so very snug!

I can show I care by
Giving you a kiss,
For showing someone that you care
A kiss can never miss!

AFTER

• **Little Mouse's Big Valentine** *by Thacher Hurd*

◄ Read *Little Mouse's Big Valentine* by Thacher Hurd with the children.

For My Valentine

BEFORE

◄ Tradition requires that we give something to the one special person we've chosen to be our "Valentine." Some of the traditional gifts are listed below.

◄ Talk to the children about the characteristics of each of the gifts, especially the last item on the list. When you give someone your "heart," what does that actually mean?

DURING

◄ Ask the children to pretend to be the following gifts. Explain that you don't want to see just the *shape* of these things, but you want to see the items actually *doing* something that typifies them.

◄ Leave the choice of action to the children or make the suggestions offered in parentheses.

◄ Valentine's Day gifts can include these things:
  • A rose (blooming)
  • A balloon (floating)
  • A box of candy (opening)
  • A card (opening)
  • A ring (shining)
  • Your heart (beating)

AFTER

◄ With the children, visit a local card store, candy store, or florist's shop to talk with the proprietors about this holiday. What is involved in getting ready for it? What is it like the day before, as well as the day itself?

July 4, 1776

Learning Objective
- *To help the children understand this holiday more fully*
- *To foster appreciation of the reason for the celebration*

BEFORE
- *Index cards with a 1, 4, 6, or 7 written on each one*

◄ Explain to the children that on July 4, 1776, America won its independence from England. We have been celebrating Independence Day on the Fourth of July ever since.

◄ Also mention that July is the seventh month of the year, and post the numbers 1, 4, 6, and 7 where the children can see them. (Writing a date in numbers may be a bit abstract for the children, but the experience with numbers and their shapes is what matters here.)

DURING

◄ Ask each child to show you the number 7 (for the month of July) with his body. Give them enough time to explore the possibilities, and then ask them to move slightly to their left (if standing, they can take a step to the left; if lying down, they can roll).

◄ Now ask each child to show you a number 4, followed by another move to the left. Can they make a number 1? How about a number 7 again? (Each number is followed by a move to the left.)

◄ Can they find another way to make a number 7? Finally, ask them to move left once again and to show you a number 6. Now congratulate them—they've just made July 4, 1776!

ALSO

◄ Divide the children into groups of four and assign each child a number (1, 7, 7, and 6). Then, ask the children in each group to arrange themselves to form "1776."

AFTER
- **Who Belongs Here? An American Story** *by Margy Burns Knight*

◄ For a thought-provoking lesson in social studies and history, read *Who Belongs Here? An American Story*, written by Margy Burns Knight.

Let's March

BEFORE

◄ Whether it's police officers in a parade or 18th century revolutionaries playing a fife and drum, marching comes to mind when we think of the Fourth of July. Talk to the children about marching and what makes someone a good marcher (a tall straight body, good rhythm, and so on).

DURING
• *Marching music*

◄ Put on a piece of marching music (John Philip Sousa marches are the most well known), and ask the children to march in the following ways:
- In place, with their knees high
- In place, turning to the right (in one direction); to the left (in the other direction)
- Forward, swinging their arms
- Pretending to play the musical instrument of their choice

AFTER
• *Rhythm band instruments*

◄ Place rhythm band instruments in the Music or Dramatic Play Center so the children can march when they want to.

The American Flag

BEFORE
◄ Talk to the children about the American flag. Do they know what colors are on it? Do they know what is on it? What do the 50 stars represent? Have the children ever seen a flag being raised up a flagpole?
◄ Discuss some of the reasons a flag might be lowered to half-mast, the proper way to fold a flag, and the respect our flag deserves.

DURING

◄ Explain to the children that they're going to pretend to be a lot of different things associated with the flag. Then ask them to show you the following:
- The shape of a flag
- A star
- A stripe
- A flagpole
- A flag being raised up a flagpole
- A flag at half-mast
- A flag waving proudly in the breeze
- A flag being lowered down a flagpole
- A flag being folded

ALSO
◄ Divide the children into "stars" and "stripes" and ask them to form either several small flags or one large one!

AFTER
• *Art materials, such as paper, markers, scissors, and glue*

◄ Provide a variety of art materials and encourage the children to create their own flags.

The Parade

BEFORE

◄ Parades are a Fourth of July tradition, and children love them! Talk to the children about the parades they've seen. Ask them:
- Who and what was in the last parade you saw?
- Were there any animals in it?
- What things did you like best?

DURING

◄ Explain to the children that they are going to pretend to be a lot of different things that might be seen in a Fourth of July parade. Use some of the ideas they discussed with you, the list below, or a combination of both.

◄ Possibilities include the following:
- A circus clown
- A soldier
- A fire engine
- A horse
- A baton twirler
- A flag bearer
- A cannon

AFTER

◄ Give the children a variety of materials to create their own components of a parade. Then, encourage them to form and hold one of their own!

Celebration!

BEFORE
◀ Discuss with the children the different ways people celebrate the Fourth of July. For example, they have barbecues, go on picnics, watch parades and fireworks, and so on. How do the children and their families like to celebrate this holiday?

DURING
◀ Ask the children to pretend to be the following things, all of which are related to the celebration of Independence Day:
- A flag being carried in a parade
- A baton being twirled
- A cannonball being fired from a cannon
- Something barbecuing on the grill
- Fireworks
- A blanket being spread for a picnic

ALSO
- *Tchaikovsky's 1812 Overture*

◀ Accompany this activity with a recording of Tchaikovsky's *1812 Overture* to add to the fun!

AFTER
◀ Invite the mayor, a selectman or selectwoman, or another local official to visit the classroom to discuss the town's plans for the holiday.

Nature

CHAPTER FIVE

Clouds

Learning Objectives
• *To familiarize children with and enhance their appreciation for various elements of nature relating to the sky*

BEFORE
◁ Ask the children for their impression of clouds:
- How many different kinds of clouds have you seen?
- What do you think clouds are made of?
- Have you ever sat looking up at the sky, watching the clouds form the shapes of objects or animals?

◁ If possible, bring the children outside after asking them these questions.

DURING
◁ Ask the children to move like the following:
- Big fluffy clouds
- Wispy clouds
- Dark storm clouds
- Clouds drifting and slowly changing shape

ALSO
◁ Ask each child to begin as a single cloud, and then gradually drift towards other children, cooperating as a group, together and apart to form larger and then smaller clouds. Sometimes two "clouds" will drift together to form a floating shape; other times, larger groups of clouds will join and separate.

AFTER
• *Art materials, such as paper, markers, scissors, and glue*

◁ On days that offer different perspectives on the sky and clouds, bring the children outside for a "cloud appreciation" period. Ask them:
- What kinds of clouds do you see?
- What color are they?
- Do any of them look like objects or animals?
- How fast, or slowly, are they moving?

◁ When the children are back indoors, provide a variety of art materials and encourage them to create their own cloud-filled skies.

Constellations

BEFORE
• *Pictures of constellations, optional*

◁ A constellation is a configuration of stars. Many constellations, to the eye or through a telescope, look like familiar shapes. Perhaps the most well known constellations are those commonly called the Big Dipper and the Little Dipper.

◁ Have the children ever seen these? If possible, provide pictures of these and other constellations.

DURING

◄ Ask the children to pretend to be stars shining in the night sky.

◄ Then call out a number (no smaller than three and no larger than six).

◄ The children divide themselves into groups of that number and form "constellations." What shapes can they make with that number of stars?

◄ Repeat this several times with different numbers. (If one or two groups are left with fewer "stars" than you've called out, that's okay. These smaller constellations can add variety to the patterns in the sky.)

AFTER

• *Art materials, such as paper, markers, scissors, and glue*

◄ If you have a planetarium nearby, arrange for a field trip.

◄ Also, encourage the children to use a variety of art materials to create their own night skies.

Over the Rainbow

BEFORE

• *Picture of a rainbow*

◄ *Webster's Third New International Dictionary* defines a rainbow as "an arc of a circle exhibiting in concentric bands the several colors of the spectrum and formed opposite the sun by the refraction and reflection of the sun's rays in drops of rain."

◄ But to most of us, a rainbow is something wonderful and colorful that sometimes appears in the sky following a rainstorm.

◄ Have the children ever seen a rainbow, either in pictures or in the sky? What shape was it? What colors were in it?

◄ Show the children a picture of a rainbow.

DURING

◄ Ask the children to each make the shape of a rainbow.

◄ Then ask them to take partners and make a two-person rainbow. Can they make rainbows standing up and lying down?

◄ Finally, ask them to join together as a group to form the biggest, most beautiful rainbow ever!

AFTER

- *Art materials, such as paper, markers, scissors, and glue*

◁ This topic definitely lends itself to an art experience!

The Solar System

BEFORE

- *Pictures of the solar system, scraps of paper, markers, and a container*

◁ Talk to the children about our solar system, which includes nine planets that revolve around the sun. They are (in the order of their distance from the sun from nearest to farthest): Mercury, Venus, Earth, Mars, Jupiter, Saturn, Uranus, Neptune, and Pluto. Our solar system also consists of the planets' moons (our planet has only one) and stars.

◁ If desired, show the children pictures of the planets and discuss the characteristics of each. Also, discuss solar and lunar eclipses, which are described in this activity.

◁ For this activity, you'll need as many scraps of paper as there are children in your group. On each piece of paper, write the name of a planet or sun, moon, or star and place them in a container.

DURING

◁ Ask each child to select one scrap of paper from the container. Then they will form a "solar system."

◁ The sun, of course, will be in the center, "radiating light." The planets should each revolve around the sun at an appropriate distance (for example, Mercury will be the closest and Pluto the farthest away). The stars should "twinkle," and the moon revolves around the earth (from west to east, if you can work that into the activity). When the moon blocks the sun, a solar eclipse occurs; when the moon is in the earth's shadow, that's a lunar eclipse. How do the children want to depict solar and lunar eclipses?

◁ (All this will take some time to work out, and it will take many repetitions before they perform it smoothly!)

AFTER

- **Space Songs for Children** *by Tonja Evetts Weimer*

◁ Play selections from Tonja Evetts Weimer's *Space Songs for Children,* a cassette with twelve songs written from a child's perspective. The accompanying book offers suggestions for related activities to extend the ideas in each song. You can also place the tape in the Music Center so the children can listen whenever they want.

Sunrise/Sunset

BEFORE

◄ Talk to the children about the rising and setting of the sun. Have they ever watched a sunrise or sunset?

◄ Explain that the sun rises in the east and sets in the west, and it takes from early morning to early evening (and sometimes longer) for the sun to move from east to west. (If the children are old enough to understand, you can explain that the sun doesn't actually move; instead, the earth revolves around *it*.)

DURING

◄ Ask each child to get into a very small shape on one side of the room (the eastern side, if possible).

◄ Then they pretend to be the sun *slowly* rising over the horizon.

◄ Once they have fully risen, the sun moves *in very slow motion*—shining all the time—across the "sky" (to the other side of the room) and begins setting, until it's no longer in sight.

ALSO

◄ If desired, accompany this activity with a piece of slow, soft music to help set the mood and tempo. And because this is a great winding down activity, you can use it any time you feel the children need to relax a bit.

AFTER

◄ Teach the children to sing "You Are My Sunshine."

WEATHER

Learning Objectives
• *To familiarize the children with and enhance their appreciation for various aspects of the weather*
• *To make frightening aspects seem less so*

Lightning and Thunder

BEFORE

◄ What do the children think about thunder and lightning? Do they find them scary? Do they like to listen and watch during a thunderstorm from within the safety of their homes?

◄ If the children are old enough to understand, you may want to explain that lightning is the flash of light caused by a discharge of electricity from one cloud to another or from a cloud to earth. Thunder is the sound that follows the lightning and is caused by the expansion of air due to the electrical discharge. Although the children won't understand it technically, knowing that the phenomena have a scientific explanation may help alleviate any fear they have.

◄ Explain to the children that flashes of lightning and rumbles of thunder can vary in intensity. Similarly, the number of seconds that pass between a flash of lightning and a rumble of thunder can also vary.

DURING

◄ Ask the children to choose a partner. The partners then decide who will be the thunder and who will be the lightning.

◄ At a signal from you, the partners separate and begin moving about the room. While moving, however, thunder must be watchful of her partner because she never knows when lightning will "strike." Every time lightning does strike, thunder must follow. In other words, the partner acting as lightning can choose any moment to "strike" (to move like lightning). The partner acting as thunder must then respond, moving in a way she feels depicts thunder.

◄ After a while, the partners reverse roles.

AFTER
• *Variety of drums*

◄ Place a variety of drums (homemade and purchased) in the Music Center so the children can have an opportunity to create various thunder sounds.

The Wind

BEFORE

◄ Talk to the children about the wind and its varying forces. A gentle breeze barely stirs the leaves on the trees, and a light steady wind can offer relief on a hot day. A heavier wind can cause the trees to sway, and finally, a gale wind (as occurs during a hurricane) can cause major damage, including uprooting trees.

DURING

◄ Ask the children to move as though they are a very gentle breeze. Then the breeze becomes a light wind.

◄ And, *gradually,* the strength of the wind grows stronger, until it's gale force.

◄ The process then slowly reverses, until the children are once again pretending to be a breeze.

ALSO

◄ After the children have experienced the varying forces required by the first activity, ask them to stand in a line, side-by-side.

◄ The first child begins as a gentle breeze, and each child down the line depicts a wind of slightly greater force, so that the last child in line is portraying a gale wind. Then, ask them to reverse the process.

◄ If time allows, ask the first child to begin as the gale wind, so the children have a chance to experience the element of force differently.

◄ Because this exercise is executed sequentially, much like a "wave" performed by fans at a sporting event, you may have to offer some assistance, depending upon the developmental level of the children.

◄ If the children have difficulty moving sequentially on their own, you can start at the beginning of the line, walking slowly toward the end, cuing each child in turn.

AFTER
• *Kites or scarves (or pieces of cloth)*

◄ On a windy day, bring the children outside for some kite flying!

◄ Or, give each child a chiffon scarf. Encourage them to discover the magic of the wind.

Dance of the Snowflakes

BEFORE

◄ Most children are fascinated by snow—even if they've never seen it. Discuss the properties of snow with the children, such as how no two snowflakes are ever alike, how snowflakes swirl in the wind, how they melt at first when falling upon a warmer earth, and how they begin to accumulate.

◄ Ask the children:
  - What do you think about snow?
  - What do you like best about it?
  - If you've never seen it, how do you imagine it to be?

DURING

◄ Read the following poem to the children while they sit and listen.

◄ Then read it again slowly, asking the children to act out the images in each verse.

> **Dance of the Snowflakes**
>
> Snowflakes drifting from the sky,
> Dancing lightly in the air.
> Falling, falling without a sound;
> Each is unique and rare.
>
> Snowflakes swirling in the wind
> In a dance they can't control.
> Higher, lower, around and 'round,
> Shivering in the cold.
>
> Snowflakes landing on the earth,
> Melting quietly from sight.
> Falling, falling until the ground
> Is blanketed in white.

AFTER
- *Cotton balls*
- *Styrofoam peanuts and a parachute*

◄ Open a couple of bags of cotton balls and encourage the children play in the "snow!" Or place cotton balls or Styrofoam peanuts on a parachute and encourage the children to create a "snowstorm" by bouncing the cotton balls or peanuts up and down on the parachute.

The Rain

BEFORE

◀ Rainfall, like the wind, has varying degrees of force. A mist of rain is barely visible and gives the impression only that the air is moist. A drizzle is somewhat more evident than a mist, and a sprinkle is even more visible.

◀ Talk to the children about rain, discussing everything from a mist to a torrential downpour. Which of the following have they actually seen?

DURING

◀ Ask the children to depict the following:
  - A mist
  - A drizzle
  - A sprinkle
  - Big heavy raindrops that plop
  - Wind-driven rain
  - A downpour
  - Rain moving across a lake

ALSO

◀ Just as you did for The Wind (page 105), ask the children to stand in line and sequentially depict rainfall, from a mist to a torrential downpour and the reverse. (Obviously rainfall will require different movements than wind.)

AFTER

◀ Teach the children "Rain, Rain Go Away," challenging them to make up new lyrics that *welcome* the rain.

The Weather Report

BEFORE

◄ Do the children ever listen to the weather report on television or the radio? Has bad weather ever changed or interrupted their plans?

◄ The weather report, which is sometimes wrong and sometimes right, predicts many different occurrences that can vary according to the area.

◄ Discuss with the children all of the weather elements listed below. The children may have already experienced some of them; however, others will be new and may require explanation.

DURING

◄ Ask the children to move like each of the following elements of the weather:
  • Steady rain
  • Sunshine
  • A hurricane
  • Freezing cold
  • Fog rolling in
  • Sleet
  • Hail
  • A tornado
  • Heat lightning
  • The 3 H's: hot, humid, and hazy

AFTER

• **Energy from the Sun** *by Allan Fowler*

◄ Read *Energy from the Sun* by Allan Fowler to the children.

It's a Bird's Life

BEFORE
◀ While all of the children have seen birds, they may not have paid particular attention to their habits. Talk to the children about the activities listed below, describing them in as much detail as possible. Have the children ever witnessed birds doing any of these things?

DURING
◀ Reminding the children that birds don't have hands, ask them to pretend to be birds doing the following:
  • Splashing in a bird bath
  • Eating seed at a feeder
  • Cracking a sunflower seed on a branch
  • Building a nest
  • Feeding a baby bird
  • Flying south
  • Sleeping in a nest

AFTER
◀ Bring the children outside to go bird watching! How many different kinds, sizes, and colors of birds can they find?

Woody Woodpecker

BEFORE
• *Photo of a woodpecker*

◀ If the children are familiar with the cartoon character Woody Woodpecker, then they should have an idea of what a woodpecker looks like. (Woody, with his famous red crest and familiar call, is based on the large, seldom seen, pileated woodpecker; but there are several other kinds of woodpeckers as well.

◀ If the children don't know who Woody Woodpecker is, show them a photo of a woodpecker—preferably one that is clinging to a tree, ready to do what it's named for.

◀ Explain to the children that woodpeckers use their very strong beaks to peck at the bark or wood of trees for two reasons: to drill for insects to eat and to dig holes for their nests. Have they ever seen or heard a woodpecker pecking at a tree? It's very rhythmic and makes a fairly loud sound.

DURING
◀ This exercise offers an opportunity for the children to practice with rhythms and with their listening skills.

◀ Explain to them that they are going to pretend to be woodpeckers drilling at trees, and they will "peck" in echoing response to the rhythms you establish. For example, if you clap three times at a slow tempo, each child uses her head to peck three times at the same tempo, saying aloud, "Peck, peck, peck."

◀ Repeat each pattern at least once, at a slightly faster tempo.

◀ Choose rhythm groupings according to the age and experience of the children in your class. Generally speaking, the younger the group, the shorter and slower the rhythms should be.

AFTER
• *Wooden blocks and striking tools*

◀ Put different sized wooden blocks in the Dramatic Play Center, with a variety of striking tools. How many different sounds can the children create?

The Hummingbird

BEFORE
• *Picture of a hummingbird, if possible*

◀ The ruby-throated hummingbird, which is the smallest bird, is the only bird that can fly backward as well as hover, like an insect, in one spot.

◀ Hummingbirds are constantly in motion, perching only briefly to rest or when they're at the nest. Hummingbirds got their name because while they are flying, their wings make humming sounds.

◀ They feed at large tubular flowers, among others, and are also attracted to feeders filled with sugar water.

◀ If possible, show the children a picture of a hummingbird.

DURING
◀ Ask the children to perform the following actions as a hummingbird would. Because the hummingbird's wings are always in motion—and move very swiftly—include pauses on twigs or at the nest between the activities below, or when you sense the "hummingbirds" need a brief rest.
• Flit from flower to flower
• Fly backward
• Drink from a feeder
• Hover

AFTER
• *Hummingbird feeder*

◀ If you live in an area with hummingbirds, prepare a feeder to place outside a window. The formula is one part sugar to four parts water.

Wise Old Owl

BEFORE

◄ Show the children a picture of an owl and talk about its characteristics. Point out the owl's short crooked beak, its large bright eyes, and the sharp talons it uses to grip the tree branches on which it perches.

◄ Other traits you might point out are the owl's ability to swivel its head and the fact that it's mostly nocturnal.

◄ Also, be sure to mention that the owl has a reputation for being very wise and that its call sounds like a "who-o-o."

DURING

◄ Ask the children to sit in a circle.

◄ Choose one child to be the "wise owl," and ask her to close her eyes and pretend to be perched on a tree limb.

◄ Once the owl's eyes are closed, point to another child who must leave the circle and hide in a predetermined place.

◄ When that child is hidden, the owl opens its big eyes, looks around, and chants:

> **Wise Old Owl**
> *Who, who, who is missing?*
> *Whoever could it be?*
> *[Child's name]—that's who's missing*
> *My wise old eyes can see!*

◄ Repeat the activity until every child has had a chance to be the owl.

ALSO

◄ If the group is too small to make the above activity challenging—or if you'd simply like another option—ask the children to identify a missing object.

◄ Place several items in the middle of the circle, pointing to and naming each one (the younger the children, the fewer the items you should select).

◄ Then, once the appointed owl has closed its eyes, remove one item and place it behind your back.

◄ Of course, then the owl will substitute "what" for "who" when chanting, but that's okay!

AFTER
• **Who's Hiding Here?** *by Yoshi*

◄ Read *Who's Hiding Here?* by Yoshi with the children. It has an owl in it, as well as the concept of something being hidden (which relates to the activities above).

The Early Bird

BEFORE
- *Pictures of various birds, if possible*

◄ "The early bird catches the worm" is a common saying that actually has nothing to do with birds. While some birds eat worms, others feast on a variety of other delicacies, from thistle to fish to snakes.

◄ Talk to the children about the following birds and their feeding habits, showing pictures whenever possible:
- Pigeons can often be found in parks, eating breadcrumbs tossed to them by their human friends.
- Kingfishers are pigeon-sized and hover or perch over water until a fish is visible. They then dive straight down for their prey.
- There are several different kinds of hawks, but many of them feed on mice, snakes, and frogs. Some sit quietly on a low perch, waiting for their prey and then dropping down swiftly. Others soar over open country and then swoop down once they've spotted prey.
- Baby birds of all kinds wait in their nests—sometimes not very patiently— for their mother or father to bring them food (usually insects). They then open their beaks as wide as possible so the parent can drop in food.
- Many tree-clinging birds, such as some woodpeckers, nuthatches, and creepers, move up and down the trunk of a tree, probing the bark for insects.
- Robins (properly called American robins) can often be seen foraging on the ground for worms.

DURING
◄ Ask the children to portray each of these birds in search of food. Feel free to add any others that come to mind.

AFTER
- *Picture of a bird nest, or a real one*
- *Art materials, such as paper, markers, scissors, and glue*

◄ Show the children a picture of a bird nest or a real one, if possible. Then, encourage them to create their own nest using a variety of art materials.

Water, Water Everywhere

Learning Objectives
• To promote awareness of and appreciation and respect for various aspects of nature

BEFORE
◄ Humans tend to have a fascination with water. We like to ride on it, play in it, and just sit and look at it. This activity focuses on the many forms of water that haven't already been covered in previous chapters.
◄ Talk to the children about the list below. Discuss the characteristics of each form of water as well as the similarities and differences between them.

DURING
◄ Ask the children to move as though they were the following:
- A babbling brook
- A winding river
- River rapids
- A waterfall
- A lawn sprinkler
- A water hose
- A geyser
- A choppy lake
- A calm lake

AFTER
- *Things that float and things that sink, and a water table*

◄ At the water table, give the children a variety of items and challenge them to find three that float. (Make sure there are at least three possibilities.)

To Bee or Not to Bee

BEFORE
◄ *Pollination* is a concept a bit too advanced for young children to grasp. However, they can understand that bees feed on the pollen and nectar in flowers and plants.
◄ Explain that as bees move from flower to flower and plant to plant, they spread the pollen with their bodies, which helps the plants and flowers grow. They also use the nectar on which they feed to produce honey.
◄ Therefore, bees are extremely helpful insects. (Perhaps that knowledge will help alleviate any fear of bees the children may have.)

DURING

◄ Teach the children the following, sung to the tune of "Row, Row, Row Your Boat."

◄ Then ask them to sing it as they pretend to be bees.

> **To Bee or Not to Bee**
> *Buzz, buzz, buzz around*
> *From plant to flower to tree;*
> *Spreading pollen everywhere,*
> *That is my job, you see.*
>
> *Buzz, buzz, buzz around,*
> *It's time to make honey.*
> *That's the very useful life*
> *Of a busy bee!*

AFTER
* *Rimsky-Korsakov's* **Flight of the Bumblebee**

◄ Introduce the children to Rimsky-Korsakov's *Flight of the Bumblebee,* which is a wonderful piece of classical music. The children can pretend to be bees as it plays, or they can simply listen.

Mountain, Mountain, Volcano

BEFORE
* *Pictures of volcanoes, optional*

◄ A volcano is a hill or mountain composed partly or completely of molten or hot rock, which flows, along with steam, from a vent in the earth's crust. Lava is the fluid rock that is spewed when a volcano erupts. A volcano often has a depression or crater at its top. Vesuvius is probably the most famous volcano in history, and Mt. St. Helens is probably the best-known volcano in North America.

◄ Show the children pictures of volcanoes, if possible. Ask them for their impressions of what happens when a volcano erupts.

DURING

◄ This activity is somewhat similar to "Duck, Duck, Goose." However, instead of tapping the children's heads and saying "duck" or "goose," you will say either "mountain" or "volcano." But that's where the similarity ends, because in this activity, there is no chasing or elimination.

◀ Ask the children to scatter on the floor and form the shapes of mountains. Ask them to close their eyes and keep them closed until they're designated to be a volcano.

◀ Then tiptoe quietly among the children, tapping each one on the head and saying either "mountain" or "volcano." The mountains will remain as they are. The volcanoes, however, will "erupt" (right where they are). After erupting, each volcano turns into lava, which spews from the crater and flows to the ground.

◀ Vary the number of mountains you designate between volcanoes so the children never know when to expect to be the latter, continuing with the activity until everyone has had a chance to "erupt."

AFTER

• *Art materials, such as paper, markers, scissors, and glue*

◀ Teach the children "The Bear Went Over the Mountain." Or provide a variety of art materials and ask them to create their own mountains and volcanoes.

Fire

BEFORE

◀ Fire is a natural wonder that has certainly proven to be both helpful and harmful. Talk to the children about the many uses of fire (such as cooking, heating homes, and campfires) and about its potential dangers (for example, getting burned with matches, homes and buildings burning, and forest fires).

◀ Also discuss fire's characteristics, such as its color(s), "size," and movement.

DURING

◀ Ask the children to move as though they were the following:
  • A match being struck
  • The flickering flame of a candle
  • A campfire
  • A flame being raised and lowered on a gas stove
  • A bonfire
  • A fire spreading
  • A forest fire out of control
  • A flame dying out

AFTER

◀ Take the children on a field trip to the local fire station, or invite a firefighter to come in and discuss fire safety.

Reptiles and Amphibians

BEFORE

◄ A reptile is an animal that crawls or moves on its belly, such as a snake, or on small short legs, such as a lizard. An amphibian lives both in and out of the water (for example, a frog).

◄ Many adults aren't particularly crazy about reptiles and amphibians, but children tend to be attracted to them.

◄ Talk to the children about snakes, lizards, and frogs. What do they think about these creatures?

◄ If they don't know what a lizard looks like, show them a picture, if possible. If you don't have a picture, describe lizards to them, perhaps using dinosaurs as a basis for comparison.

DURING

◄ Ask the children to pretend to be snakes, lizards, and frogs. After they've had a chance to experiment on their own, make various suggestions for movement.

◄ Possibilities include the following:
   • Catching an insect with a flick of the tongue
   • A snake wrapping itself around the limb of a tree
   • A frog swimming
   • A frog jumping from one lily pad in a pond to another
   • A lizard hiding under a rock

ALSO

◄ Leap Frog is an age-old game that has never lost its appeal for children. Why not play a game with the children and give them further cause to think about frogs?

AFTER
• **Froggie Went A 'Courtin' by Chris Conover**

◄ Teach the children the song "The Frog Went A-Courtin'." (*Froggie Went A 'Courtin'*, a book by Chris Conover, is an illustrated version of the song.)

◄ If you live in an area with any of these creatures around, bring the children outside to search for them—for viewing only, of course.

Animals

CHAPTER SIX

It's a Dog's Life

Learning Objectives
• *To help children consider and more fully appreciate the role of pets in our lives*
• *To foster greater respect for domestic animals*

BEFORE

◁ It's very likely that all the children are familiar with dogs. Discuss various canine traits and the way dogs move when they perform the activities listed below.

DURING

◁ Stressing realism, ask the children to show you how a dog moves when it does the following:

- Wags its tail
- Fetches a newspaper
- Shakes hands
- Buries a bone
- Begs
- Plays catch with a Frisbee
- Rolls over

AFTER
- **Cats Do, Dogs Don't by Norma Simon**

◁ Read *Cats Do, Dogs Don't* by Norma Simon. Also, ask those children who have dogs at home to bring in pictures, or to tell the class about them.

Pretty Birdie

BEFORE

◁ Talk to the children about the various kinds of birds that can be pets and about the pleasures involved in owning a bird.
◁ Ask the children:
- Do you have birds at home?
- Can you describe them for the class?
- What kinds of things do the birds do?

DURING

◁ Ask the children to show you how a bird performs the following:
- Swinging on its swing
- Eating birdseed
- Looking at itself in the mirror
- Flapping its wings
- Flying
- Singing

AFTER

◄ Teach the children the following song, sung to the melody of "Twinkle, Twinkle, Little Star."

Pretty Birdie

Pretty birdie on your swing,
How I love to hear you sing.
With your feathers oh-so-bright
You can make my cares seem light.
Pretty birdie on your swing,
How I love to hear you sing!

BEFORE

◄ Although there are a number of characteristics considered typical of felines, cats, like people, all have personalities distinctly their own. Do the children have cats at home? What kind of personalities do they have? How do they move when they behave in the ways listed below?

DURING

◄ Stressing realism, ask the children to show you how a cat moves when it is behaving in the following ways:
- Playing with a toy
- Being affectionate
- Stalking prey
- Cleaning itself
- Rubbing against furniture
- Being afraid of something
- Curling up to go to sleep
- Being lazy

AFTER

- ***Books about cats, such as* Where Does My Cat Sleep? *by Norma Simon,* Have You Seen My Cat? *by Eric Carle, and* Millions of Cats *by Wanda Gag**

◄ There is no shortage of stories about cats to read with the children. Among them are Norma Simon's *Where Does My Cat Sleep?*, Eric Carle's *Have You Seen My Cat?*, and Wanda Gag's *Millions of Cats*. Also, invite the children with cats at home to bring in pictures.

BEFORE
* *Pictures of turtles, optional*

◁ Turtles are special animals. They are among the slowest of creatures, and they have the ability to pull their bodies inside their shells. If possible, show the children a picture of a turtle, then discuss turtles and their characteristics. Have the children ever seen or had a turtle? How did it move?

◁ Moving slowly is not an easy task for young children, as it requires a great deal of control. However, because pretending comes naturally to them, exploring the movements of a turtle provides them with an excellent opportunity to practice slow-motion moving.

DURING
◁ Ask the children to assume the shape of a turtle and show you how a turtle hides inside its shell.

◁ Then ask them to come out of their "shells" and show you how slowly a turtle moves. (You may want to designate beginning and ending points for them. But emphasize that they are to reach the "finish line" *slowly.*)

◁ If you have an especially competitive class, you might ask them to show you which "turtle" can move the slowest. (Be sure to offer praise and congratulations to all the turtles!)

AFTER
* *Art materials, such as paper, markers, scissors, and glue*

◁ Give the children a variety of art materials and ask them to create their own turtles. How do they want to decorate their shells?

If I Could Have Any Pet I Want

BEFORE
◁ With this activity, stress the importance of choosing a pet carefully. Talk to the children about the pets mentioned in the poem below (and others, if you'd like). Discuss both the responsibilities and joys involved in having them.

◁ Ask the children:
  * Do you have any pets at home?
  * Do you help take care of them?
  * What are some of your pets' most predominant characteristics?
  * How do your pets move?

DURING

◄ Read the following poem slowly, giving the children ample time to pretend to be the animal discussed in each verse.

◄ Because there are several pets mentioned in the fifth verse, read it even slower than the others.

◄ For the last verse, the children can simply listen, recite the lines with you, or move like their favorite pets.

If I Could Have Any Pet I Want

If I could have any pet I want,
It'd be so hard to choose—
I'd like to have a puppy dog,
But he might chew up my shoes!

I'd like to have a furry kitten
Who would snuggle up and purr,
But then I know that come the spring
She would start to shed her fur!

Maybe tropical fish would be nice—
I'd watch them swim all day.
But I might have to clean their tank
When I'd rather go and play!

A hamster, a gerbil, or a mouse
Might make a real good pet.
But if it happened to get sick
Could I take it to the vet?

Still, puppies are fun, and loving, too;
Tropical fish are pretty.
Hamsters, gerbils, and mice are cute,
And I would love a kitty!

Yes, it might be work to have a pet,
But they sure are lots of fun.
They also make the best of friends—
So why not have more than one?!

AFTER

• Music about animals

◄ To add mathematics to the activity, ask the children to vote for their favorite pet.

◄ To contribute musical experiences, choose selections from such albums as *Animal Antics, Animal Walks,* and *Walk Like the Animals.*

◄ To help children realize the responsibility involved in choosing and having a pet, take a field trip to the local humane society.

Learning Objectives
• *To familiarize the children with forest animals and their environment*
• *To foster respect and compassion for these creatures*

Skunks, Raccoons, and Foxes

BEFORE
• *Pictures of skunks, raccoons, and foxes, optional*

◄ Showing the children pictures of skunks, raccoons, and foxes would be very helpful. However, if you don't have pictures available, you can describe these animals to the children. (The children have probably seen at least one of these animals.)

◄ Focus especially on the skunk's odor, which it uses to deter potential enemies; the raccoon's mask, which makes the animal look like a bandit; and the fox's beautiful, long, fluffy tail.

DURING

◄ Explain to the children that every time you say the word "skunks," they should hold their noses. When you say "raccoons," they should make a mask over their eyes with their hands. And when you say "foxes," they should make a tail with one or both arms.

◄ Begin chanting these three words very slowly at first, giving the children time to get used to the activity. Then, gradually pick up the pace. The faster you go, the more confusing—and fun—it will become!

◄ If you have a very young group of children, saying the animal's names in the same order every time will create less confusion. However, with an older group (or a young group that's repeated this activity often), mix it up by sometimes saying the names in the same order and sometimes not.

AFTER
• *Art materials, such as paper, markers, scissors, and glue*

◄ Give the children a variety of art materials and encourage them to create one or more of these creatures.

The Bear

BEFORE

◄ Have any of the children ever seen a bear, perhaps at a zoo? Explain that you're not talking about polar bears, which live in arctic regions, but about the kinds of bears that live in forests.

◀ Discuss all of the habits listed below, talking especially about the movement involved. For instance, a bear doesn't climb a tree like a person does. Instead, the bear generally alternates its front and back legs to shimmy up a tree.

DURING

◀ Ask the children to pretend to be bears performing the following activities:
- Walking on four legs
- Walking on hind legs
- Climbing a tree
- Crossing a fallen tree trunk
- Catching a fish in a river
- Shaking water from its coat
- Sleeping in its cave

AFTER

- *Books about bears, such as* **The Valentine Bears** *by Eve Bunting,* **Jesse Bear, What Will You Wear?** *by Nancy White Carlstrom, and* **Jamberry** *by Bruce Degen*

◀ There is no shortage of books to read about bears! Among the possibilities are *The Valentine Bears* by Eve Bunting, *Jesse Bear, What Will You Wear?* by Nancy White Carlstrom, and *Jamberry* by Bruce Degen.

The Deer and the Moose

BEFORE

- *Pictures of deer and moose*

◀ Although they are members of the same family, there are some differences between deer and moose, the most notable being size. Also, while all moose have antlers, not all deer do. Most male deer have antlers, but only a few types of females do.

◀ Show the children pictures of a deer and a moose, and talk to them about the differences between them.

DURING

◀ Explain to the children that as you read this playfully "argumentative" poem, they will alternate between pretending to be a moose and a deer.

◀ Every time they hear the word *moose*, they should make themselves as large as possible and use their hands to demonstrate antlers.

◀ When they hear the word *deer*, they should make themselves smaller and use a hand or hands to show the deer's tail.

- On the final two lines, the children should don "horns" and "run away."
- If you can, speak in two different voices, pretending to be the "debaters" quoted in the poem to ensure even greater enjoyment for the children.
- Also, with subsequent repetitions of this activity, read the poem more and more quickly, making it increasingly challenging!

The Deer and the Moose

I just saw a deer behind that tree
And don't you know she was looking at me!
That was no deer—it's plain to see
That was a moose, as big as can be!

A deer, I say, with a tail of white
And eyes that shine in the dark of night!
It was a moose, I'm sure I'm right—
The animal had tremendous height!

A deer or a moose—what silly chatter;
The deer is smaller; the moose is fatter.
The moose has antlers like a ladder;
The deer moves softly, pitter-patter!

Well, you must agree we will never know
Gigantic bull moose or spotted doe.
It could have been a buffalo
Whatever it was left long ago!

AFTER
• *Paper and pen or marker*

- Ask the children to name all the differences and similarities between a deer and a moose. Write down their responses.

BEFORE
- Technically, to hop on two feet is to *jump* (hopping is performed on one foot at a time). Yet, when we think in terms of bunnies and rabbits, we think of their method of locomotion as hopping.
- With this activity, you're going to ask the children to, among other things, move like rabbits. It will be up to them whether they want to move on two feet or on "all fours."
- Talk to the children about rabbits. Discuss their traits and the way they move. What do rabbits look like?

DURING

◁ Ask the children to show you the following:
   • Rabbit ears
   • A rabbit's tail
   • A rabbit wiggling its nose
   • A rabbit eating lettuce
   • A rabbit washing its face

◁ Now ask the children to show you how a rabbit moves. Encourage them to occasionally stop and sniff the air (for food, or the possibility of danger!).
◁ When the children have moved long enough, ask them to show you a rabbit ducking into its hole in the ground.

AFTER

◁ Read Margaret Wise Brown's classic story, *The Runaway Bunny,* or the newer *Rebecca Rabbit Plays Hide-and-Seek* by Evelien van Dort.

Dance of the Animals

BEFORE
• *Pictures of various forest animals*
• *A recording of lively music*

◁ So far, the children have pretended to be rabbits, bears, raccoons, skunks, foxes, deer, and moose. Review the characteristics of these animals and then talk about others that live in forests, providing pictures whenever possible.
◁ Other forest animals might include squirrels, chipmunks, snakes, mice, and moles.
◁ Choose a recording of a lively, upbeat piece of music.

DURING

◁ Ask the children to choose the forest animal they would most like to be.
◁ Then put on the recording of lively, upbeat music and ask the children to move like the animals they represent (or to dance like they think the animals would).

ALSO

◁ Another option is to play Statues, randomly stopping and starting the music and asking the children to move only while the music is playing.
◁ When the music stops, they must freeze into statues of

their animals.

◄ If you choose this activity, you might want to assign one animal to the entire group for each segment of music. For example, before the music begins, ask the children to move like bears.

◄ Then, when the music stops, they must freeze like bears.

◄ Before the music starts again, ask them to move next like raccoons, and so on.

AFTER
• *Art materials, such as paper, markers, scissors, and glue*

◄ Encourage the children to use the art materials to create their favorite forest animal.

◄ Or, for a mathematics experience, ask the children to vote for their favorite forest animal.

◄ Read *Chipmunk Song* by Joanne Ryder or *Squirrels* by Brian Wildsmith to the children.

This Little Piggy

BEFORE

◄ Talk to the children about pigs and their characteristics. Discuss such common traits as their habit of rolling in the mud, their weight, their short legs, their curly tails, and the sounds they make (snorts and grunts, as well as oinks). You can also mention that they eat side-by-side at a trough.

DURING

◄ Give the children a chance to briefly experiment moving like pigs. (Remind them to keep the pigs' heaviness in mind.)

◄ Then, ask them to remain "in character" and move appropriately to the challenges below.

◄ These challenges come in the form of the chant: "This little piggy…," with the line completed by one of the following possibilities:
  • Rolled in the mud
  • Ate dinner
  • Went for a walk
  • Called to a friend
  • Lay down

AFTER

◄ Ask the children for suggestions of additional ways to end the phrase: "This little piggy…"

Horseplay

BEFORE

◄ This activity provides an opportunity to introduce, or practice, the locomotor skill of galloping. Performed with an uneven rhythm, the gallop calls for one foot to lead, with the other playing "catch-up."

◄ Although a child will first learn to gallop with the dominant foot forward, he should eventually also learn to execute the gallop with his nondominant foot leading.

◄ Before introducing this skill, talk to the children about horses and how they move. Have the children ever seen horses? How do they look when they're running?

DURING

◄ Demonstrate galloping for those children who don't yet know how to gallop, helping those who need extra assistance by holding their hands and galloping beside them.

◄ Naturally, not all of the children will master this skill the first day they try, so you should ask the children to perform the following by simply asking them to "move like a horse does." That way, all the children have a chance to succeed!

- Challenges include moving in the following ways:
  - Forward
  - In a circle
  - In a curving path
  - In a zigzag path
  - Occasionally leaping a fence
  - Stopping for a drink of water

AFTER
- **Stick horses**

- Provide stick horses so the children can practice galloping—and pretending—whenever the urge strikes!

Which Came First?

BEFORE
- It's an age-old question: Which came first, the chicken or the egg? Though the children may not have an opinion when you first ask them, they may after you've had a chance to discuss the dilemma with them.
- Talk to them about where eggs (and chickens) come from. Discuss how chickens lay eggs in a nest, which hatch to reveal baby chicks. These chicks eventually grow up to lay more eggs in other nests.
- Spend some time describing the hatching process, which involves the baby chick chipping away at the shell, little by little, from the inside of the egg. Finally, when enough of the shell has been removed, the baby chick is freed, but exhausted. Therefore, it takes a while for the chick to be able to get up and move around. (Some of the children may have witnessed this process before, as many county fairs and science museums have eggs hatching under sun lamps. But if some of the children have never seen this phenomenon, try to be as detailed as possible in your description. Or provide a picture book that shows the process.)
- Also, discuss the characteristics of full-grown chickens with the children. What do chickens look like? How do they sound? How do they move? How do they eat?

DURING
- Ask the children to each pretend to be an egg in a nest. Then, as they imagine their nests getting warmer, they pretend to be baby chicks working their way out of the eggs.
- Ask them to continue with the process as you described it to them (you can narrate if you find it helpful), until they've finally grown to be adult chickens.
- At that time, they should be moving like full-grown chickens, running around the barnyard, pecking at food on the ground, clucking, and laying more eggs!

AFTER
- **Chickens Aren't the Only Ones *by Ruth Heller***

- Read Ruth Heller's *Chickens Aren't the Only Ones*, which explains that chickens aren't the only animals that lay eggs.

On the Farm

BEFORE

◄ The following poem is intended to familiarize the children with a variety of animals that might be found on a farm. Discuss the animals mentioned in the poem and discuss with the children the way each one looks and moves.

DURING

◄ Ask the children to pretend to be each of the animals written about in the following poem:

On the Farm

Waddling is the duck's own way
Of moving on the ground,
But when she moves into water
There's no better swimmer found!

Gobble, gobble, the turkey says
As he surveys the land.
He has feathers that when spread out
Look very much like a fan!

The cow just loves to chew on grass,
Then take a casual stroll.
To stroll and chew and stroll and chew
Is her one and only goal!

Kids is the name for little goats,
And they just love to play.
Climbing, leaping, butting, jumping—
That's how they spend their day!

AFTER

• **Books about farms, such as On the Farm by Frantisek Chochola or Dora Duck and the Juicy Pears by Evelien van Dort**

◄ Read the children some books about farm animals, such as Frantisek Chochola's *On the Farm*, a wordless board book, and Evelien van Dort's *Dora Duck and the Juicy Pears*.

Old MacDonald

BEFORE

◄ "Old MacDonald Had a Farm" is the perfect song for a farm animal activity. The version presented below, however, is a variation on the traditional theme. It offers an opportunity for problem solving as well as movement. Because of the experience the children have had with animals to this point, they shouldn't have any trouble with the additional challenge.

◄ Before beginning, review the animals (and their characteristics, if necessary) that might be found on a farm.

◄ Also remind the children that certain domestic animals (primarily cats and dogs) are often seen on farms.

DURING

◄ Instruct the children to each think of a farm animal they would like to be.

◄ You begin to sing, "Old MacDonald had a farm," and so on.

◄ When you get to the line, "And on his farm he had a _____," instead of singing the name of an animal, point to a child, who then imitates the actions of the animal he has chosen to be (without making any sounds).

◄ The rest of the children must guess what kind of animal the child is imitating.

◄ Once they've guessed correctly, everyone sings the song, including the name of the animal and the appropriate sound.

◄ Continue until every child has had a chance to be an animal.

◄ Tell the group that if another child portrays an animal they've chosen, they can either select another animal or perhaps find a different way to portray the same one.

AFTER

• *Art materials, such as paper, markers, scissors, and glue*

◄ Encourage the children to use a variety of art materials to create their own farms.

◄ Take a vote to determine which is the most popular farm animal.

The Elephant

BEFORE

◄ Chances are, the children have all seen elephants—at least on television. Spend some time reviewing the physical and character traits that make an elephant what it is. Emphasize the elephant's weight and its heaviness of movement.

DURING

◄ Ask the children to imagine that they are elephants and show you the following:
- An elephant walking
- Ivory tusks
- An elephant's tail swishing
- An elephant eating (using its trunk)
- Big, floppy ears
- An elephant showering (using its trunk)
- An elephant running
- An elephant lying down

AFTER
- **Stand Back, Said the Elephant, I'm Going to Sneeze** *by Patty Thomas*

◄ Read *Stand Back, Said the Elephant, I'm Going to Sneeze* by Patty Thomas to the children.

Learning Objectives
- *To acquaint children with jungle animals and their environment*
- *To alleviate any fears the children may harbor about these animals*
- *To foster greater respect for these creatures and their environment*

Monkey See, Monkey Do

BEFORE

◄ This partner activity is a variation of the Mirror Game (page 17), in which one child performs movements and the other child faces him and imitates those movements as though he were a mirror reflection.

◄ It is an excellent exercise for teaching children to perform with their bodies what their eyes are seeing.

◄ Talk to the children about mirrors and their reflections. Then talk to them about monkeys and their habit of imitating what they see. Have the children ever seen monkeys? What kinds of things do they do? (Possible answers include scratching their heads, clapping, making "monkey" sounds, and jumping up and down.)

DURING

◄ Ask the children to pair off and face one another.

◄ Pretending to be a monkey, the first child in each pair performs a movement that a monkey might do (based, for the most part, on your discussion).

◀ The second child then imitates that child's movement.

◀ After a while, ask the children to switch roles so that both have a chance to be the "leader."

AFTER

◀ Sing and act out "Three Little Monkeys." You can also play "Monkey Do," a song from Derrie Frost's *A Zippity Zoo Day*.

The Giraffe

BEFORE
• *Pictures of giraffes, optional*

◀ Ask the children if they have ever seen a giraffe. If possible, show them a picture of a giraffe. Explain that it is the tallest of all living animals. What's the giraffe's most striking feature? How do they think the giraffe would feel if it ever had a sore throat? Explain that giraffes eat leaves from the tops of trees in the jungle. (It must take a long time to swallow!) Also point out that the giraffe's front legs are longer than its back legs.

DURING

◀ Encourage the children to act like giraffes to the accompaniment of the following poem:

The Giraffe
I am tall,
As tall as can be,
I can eat
From the tops of trees!

Gulp, gulp, gulp,
I swallow my food,
Then eat more
If I'm in the mood!

I can run
With my tall front legs;
They're so long
They resemble pegs!

I can bend,
Though it takes a while;
High to low
Can feel like a mile!

AFTER
• *Measuring tapes, rulers, or other measuring devices*

◀ Invite the children to measure their own necks and then guess how long they think a giraffe's neck is!

Hippos and Rhinos

BEFORE
• *Pictures of hippos and rhinos, optional*

◀ Because children often confuse hippos and rhinos, this activity may help clarify things in their minds.

◀ If possible, show the children pictures of both a hippopotamus and a rhinoceros. Then talk about the differences between the two. The most obvious difference, of course, is that the rhino has a horn protruding from its snout. The hippo, on the other hand, has large, protruding eyes, reminiscent of a bullfrog's. With regard to their movements, rhinos generally charge, while hippos lumber.

◀ Explain to the children that the "guy" used in the following poem is just an expression, assuring them that hippos and rhinos can also be "girls."

DURING
◀ Encourage the children to act like rhinos and hippos, as appropriate, to the accompaniment of the following poem:

Hippos and Rhinos

Hippopotamus is a very strange name—
It belongs to a guy with big eyes.
And when he opens up his mouth,
You can hardly believe its size!

Rhinoceros is a very strange name—
It belongs to a guy with a horn.
And if he were not quite so short
You'd think he was a unicorn!

The hippo lumbers, and he likes to bathe;
The rhino's been known to charge.
And though they both are short and squat,
They both are really rather large!

But get them straight now in your mind,
For they are not the same.
The rhino is known for his horn;
Big eyes and mouth the hippo's fame!

AFTER
- *Art materials, such as paper, markers, scissors, and glue*

◄ Encourage the children to create hippos and rhinos using a variety of art materials.

A Photo Safari

BEFORE
◄ Hopefully, when today's children grow up, if they decide to go on safari, it will be to shoot photos of the animals and not the animals themselves. Their trophies will be albums and videotapes they can share with their friends, and not animal heads mounted on walls.

◄ Talk to the children about what a photo safari would be like—riding through the jungle in a jeep, witnessing all sorts of wild animals in their natural habitats, and capturing those sights forever on film.

◄ Also, if you are going to include in the activity any animals the children have not yet portrayed, discuss them with the children.

DURING

◄ Explain to the children that you are going to pretend to be on a safari, spotting and photographing all kinds of jungle animals. They, in turn, will pretend to be the animals.

◄ As you ready your "camera," call out the name of the animal you've spotted. The children then portray that animal.

◄ Choose from the following:
  • Lions
  • Hippos
  • Apes
  • Giraffes
  • Tigers
  • Zebras
  • Elephants
  • Gazelles
  • Rhinos
  • Chimpanzees

AFTER

• *Recording of Save the Animals, Save the Earth and an inexpensive camera*

◄ Play selections from *Save the Animals, Save the Earth*. Also, bring in an inexpensive camera so the children can practice their photography.

The Sea

CHAPTER SEVEN

OCEAN CREATURES

Learning Objectives
• To familiarize the children with ocean creatures
• To foster greater respect for these creatures and for their environment

Follow That Fish!

BEFORE

◄ Talk to the children about different kinds of fish. What was the smallest fish they ever saw? The biggest? How do fish move? What are some different things fish do? (Possibilities include jumping out of the water, eating food from the ocean floor, flapping their fins, and flipping their tails.) Explain that fish often swim together in groups, called *schools*.

DURING

◄ Choose a child to begin as "lead fish." That child starts moving about the room, pretending to be a fish (and performing fish-like movements), while the other children follow and imitate.

◄ Repeat this until every child has had a chance to lead. (If you have a large group of children, you might choose to break them up into several "schools," so there are just a few fish following each leader.)

AFTER
• **The Rainbow Fish** *by Marcus Pfister*

◄ Read the award-winning *The Rainbow Fish* with the children.

Rhythmic Lobsters

BEFORE
• Castanets, optional

◄ For this activity, it would be perfect if every child had a pair of castanets. However, if that's not possible, a little imagination will have to do as a substitute!

◄ The idea behind the activity is for the children to pretend that they're lobsters and to imagine that their hands are lobster claws.

◄ Talk to the children about what lobsters look like (especially their claws).

DURING

◄ This is a rhythm exercise. As you clap out various groupings of beats, the children will repeat them, pretending to be lobsters. For example, if you clap three times at a moderate tempo, the children will repeat those three beats with their hands, which they're holding in the air and pretending are lobster claws. Along with the movement of their hands, the children make clicking noises with their mouths (pretending that their claws are making the clicks).

◄ *Note:* You'll want to choose rhythm groupings according to the age and experience of your students. Generally speaking, the younger the children, the shorter and slower the rhythm groupings should be. For example, with very young children, you might clap two times, pausing between the first and second clap. Then, increase the challenge by clapping the same pattern at a faster tempo and, later, by increasing the number of claps.

◄ With older children (or with those who have more experience with rhythms), you can even combine groupings. For example, you might clap two times, then three times, with only a slight pause between phrases.

AFTER
• Castanets

◄ Place a pair of castanets in the Music Center so the children can follow up with their explorations.

Somewhere Deep in the Ocean

BEFORE

◄ Talk to the children about each of the animals mentioned in the poem below: dolphins, whales, sharks, and seals. Discuss the creatures' physical and character traits and the differences between the way each one moves. Have the children ever seen any of these animals? What do they remember most about them?

DURING

◄ Sing the following song to the tune of "Somewhere Over the Rainbow."

◄ Ask the children to pretend to be the animal mentioned in each verse.

Somewhere Deep in the Ocean

Somewhere deep in the ocean
A dolphin plays.
Swimming, splashing, and chatting—
That's how she spends her days!

Somewhere deep in the ocean
Whales do live.
They can be very graceful,
Even though quite massive!

Somewhere deep in the ocean
A shark roams.
It can be very scary
To come upon his home!

Somewhere deep in the ocean
Swims a seal,
Sliding throughout the blue sea
Slippery as an eel!

AFTER
• **What's in the Sea? by Lois Skiera-Zucek**

◄ Play selections from Lois Skiera-Zucek's *What's in the Sea?,* which is available from the Educational Record Center. Place it in the Music Center.

The Jellyfish

BEFORE
• *Picture of a jellyfish, optional*

◄ It would be very helpful to show the children a photo of a jellyfish. If you don't have a photo, describe a jellyfish to the children by explaining that it's the shape of a flying saucer. Also, the jellyfish is known for its fluid movement, because it is of a consistency similar to jelly! How do the children think jelly moves? Is the movement tense or relaxed?

DURING

◄ Ask the children to each assume the shape of a jellyfish, however they imagine that to be.

◄ Once they've done so, instruct them to relax various parts of their bodies, starting with their toes and moving up to their head.

◄ Then, once the children are completely relaxed, tell them that they feel just like a jellyfish does.

◄ Ask them to move in the way a jellyfish would, reminding them to continue feeling like a jellyfish.

ALSO

◄ You can use this as a relaxation exercise any time the children need to wind down a bit. After they've moved like jellyfish, ask the "jellyfish" to show you how they sleep.

AFTER
• *Ingredients and equipment to make jelly*

◄ Make jelly with the children. Or, bring some into class and explore what you can do with it besides make peanut butter and jelly sandwiches.

The Eel

BEFORE
• *Picture of an eel, optional*

◁ This is a group activity, requiring lots of cooperation. Emphasize this to the children, making success a challenge and a goal for them.

◁ Talk to the children about eels and show them a picture, if possible. Explain that eels are actually fish that look like snakes. One type of eel is the electric eel, which can grow up to six feet long and has the ability to shock in the way that electricity does.

DURING

◁ Explain to the children that, together, they're going to form a very long eel and they're going to pretend the eel is swimming in the ocean.

◁ Ask the children to begin by getting on the floor and moving individually, as they believe eels would. Then at a signal from you, one by one, they start to join together by taking hold of another child's ankles—until all the children are joined and moving like a giant eel. (If you find the indiscriminate joining to be too confusing for the children, assign one child to take the ankles of another child nearby by calling out their names.)

◁ Finally, when the children have successfully accomplished this, tell them they've become an electric eel and you've just turned on their electricity! What would that look like?

AFTER
• *Clay or playdough*

◁ Give the children clay or playdough and encourage them to create their own eels.

Things at the Beach

BEFORE

◄ This activity provides an excellent opportunity for children to explore the concepts of space and shape, which are both necessary preparation for abstract thought.

◄ Talk with the children about the things (alive and otherwise) that they see when they go to the beach. Can they describe the shapes of those things? Specifically discuss the shapes of the things listed below.

DURING

◄ Ask the children to show you the shapes of the following things, as well as those mentioned during your discussion:

- Sailboats
- Seashells
- Starfish
- Dogs
- Crabs
- Beach balls
- Surfboards
- Radios
- Sand castles
- Picnic baskets
- Frisbees
- Blankets

AFTER

◄ If you live in an area with a beach, take the children on an outing to collect seashells.

◄ Or, have a picnic (indoors or out) and pretend you're at the beach!

Learning Objectives
- *To open the children's eyes to all the beauty and fun the beach has to offer, whether they've ever been to one or not*

Beach Activities

BEFORE

◄ Ask the children to tell you what kinds of activities in which they and other people participate when they go to the beach.

DURING

◄ Ask the children to show you what it looks like to perform certain beach activities. Possibilities include:
  - Swimming
  - Jogging
  - Playing volleyball
  - Playing with a Frisbee
  - Surfing
  - Building castles in the sand
  - Playing "tag" with the waves
  - Reading a book
  - Having a barbecue
  - Taking a nap

AFTER

- *Frisbees and a variety of balls*

◄ Take Frisbees and a variety of balls outside and encourage the children to pretend that they are playing with these objects at the beach.

Sand Castles

BEFORE

- *Pictures of castles, optional*

◄ Talk to the children about castles and the various elements that make them castles (for example, towers, moats, and drawbridges). Help them to form a very clear image of a castle in their minds. If possible, show them pictures of castles.

◄ Discuss building castles in the sand. Talk about what makes a good sand castle, how the sand must be wet in order to hold together, and so on.

DURING

◄ Explain to the children that you're going to build a sand castle, and they are going to be the sand.

◄ Start by asking each of them to get into the smallest shape possible, pretending to be a tiny grain of sand. (Make sure they are in their own "personal space.")

◄ Then begin to gather the "grains of sand" together into a "lump," from which you'll shape your castle.

◄ Proceed to build the castle by asking some children to remain low to the floor—some in a circle, others forming the drawbridge.

◄ Then shape the castle itself by using the different levels in space. In other words, ask some children to kneel, others to crouch, some to stand with bended knees, and the rest to stand upright. The castle will grow taller as the children do this.

◄ Finally, a few children can pretend to be the flags waving at the top of the castle. They can stand on tiptoe, as tall as they can be, and imitate the movement of a flag in the breeze.

AFTER
• **Sand, water, sand and water table or sandbox, shovels, sand molds**

◄ Encourage the children to create sand castles at the sand table or outside in the sandbox.

Walking on the Beach

BEFORE
◄ Ask the children to tell you some of the reasons a person might walk along the beach. Some of the reasons may be for exercise, to look for seashells, to be alone to think, to feel the cool sand or water on her feet, or to walk a dog.

DURING
◄ Ask the children to show you how it would look to walk on the beach in the following ways:
  • On hot sand that burns the feet
  • With a dog on a leash
  • Through wet, sticky sand
  • Looking for shells
  • As though cold
  • As though sad
  • Briskly, for exercise
  • Pulling a kite
  • Bouncing a ball
  • Happily strolling

AFTER
- *Large map of the United States*
- *Dark marker or crayon*

◄ Place a large map on the wall and explain to the children that they are going to "walk" the shoreline along the east or west coasts.

◄ Then, take them for a walk around the building, classroom, or gymnasium. Every time you go around, use a brightly colored or dark marker or crayon to designate on a map a mile "traveled" along the chosen coastline.

◄ When you've traversed the entire coastline, start on the other one! This is a great way to promote daily physical activity, and it's also a lesson in geography.

◄ If you study each of the states traveled, it also involves social studies.

BEFORE
- *Soft music, optional*

◄ This is a great relaxation exercise, as well as an opportunity to stimulate the children's imaginations. To enhance the mood, you might want to play soft music in the background. Many of the so-called New Age recordings consist of appropriate pieces for this activity, as do a number of children's recordings for "quiet times."

◄ Talk to the children about some of the reasons people lie around on the beach (for example, to get a tan, relax, take a nap, and read). What are some of the sensations experienced when lying on the beach? What might they feel (for example, the warm sun, the cool breeze, or the softness of a blanket on the sand)? What might they hear (for example, the waves rolling in or lapping at the shore, sea gulls calling)? What might they smell? (The fresh sea air is one possibility.)

DURING

◄ Ask the children to lie on the floor, close their eyes, and imagine that they're lying on blankets at the beach.

◄ Then paint a picture of the beach in their minds. Describe, in a quiet and soothing voice, the things they might be feeling, hearing, and smelling.

AFTER
- *Art materials, such as paper, markers, scissors, and glue*
- **Three by the Sea** *by Edward Marshall*

◄ Encourage the children to use a variety of art materials to create their own beach scenes.

◄ Read them Edward Marshall's *Three by the Sea*.

Sea Gulls

BEFORE
• **Pictures of sea gulls, optional**

◄ It is the herring gull that is commonly known as the "sea gull." If possible, show the children a picture of a sea gull. Talk to the children about how sea gulls look, walk, and fly. Also, discuss the other activities listed below.

DURING

◄ Stressing realism, ask the children to pretend to be sea gulls doing the following:
- Walking the beach
- Soaring through the sky
- Diving for fish
- Dropping a clamshell onto a rock
- Riding a wave

AFTER
• *Hap Palmer's* **Sea Gulls Music for Rest and Relaxation**

◄ Play Hap Palmer's *Sea Gulls Music for Rest and Relaxation* for the children, and then place it in the Music Center.

Learning Objectives
• *To acquaint the children with certain aspects of the sea not previously explored*
• *To foster appreciation and respect for this important environment*

Rockin' the Boat

BEFORE
• **Pictures of different kinds of boats, optional**

◄ How many of the children have ever been in a boat on the ocean? What was it like? What kind of boat were they in?

◄ Discuss the different kinds of boats that might be found on the ocean. Possibilities include sailboats, motorboats, cabin cruisers, and boats that are paddled or rowed. If possible, show them pictures of different boats.

◄ Then talk about the ocean itself, such as what it's like when it's calm, when it's windy, and when there's a ferocious storm. Have the children ever seen the ocean during a storm (perhaps on television)? It almost seems as though the ocean is very angry.

DURING

◄ Ask the children to each choose the kind of boat they'd like to have. Then describe a scene to them like the one below and ask them to act it out.

It's a bright, sunny day, and you decide to take your boat out on the ocean. Off you go, into the sparkling blue water. For a while, the cruise is peaceful.

There's a gentle breeze, and the relaxing roll of the waves rocks the boat as though it were a baby's cradle.

Then, as you get further out, you notice clouds beginning to roll in. The sky goes from blue to gray, and the ocean does the same. Suddenly the gentle breeze becomes a biting wind, and the clouds open up with a downpour of slashing, wind-driven rain. Waves crash into and over your boat, drenching you. You no longer feel like a baby being rocked, but like a salad being tossed!

And, then, just as suddenly as the storm began, it starts to abate. The winds die down, the sun appears from behind a cloud, and the waves grow smaller. Your boat moves steadily again as the ocean grows calm. The sunshine dries everything off, including your wet clothes. And once more you begin to enjoy the serenity of your surroundings.

AFTER
• **Books about boats, such as Mr. Gumpy's Outing by John Burningham**

◄ Read John Burningham's *Mr. Gumpy's Outing* to the children.

Deep-Sea Diving

BEFORE
◄ Talk to the children about the many things that can be found beneath the surface of the ocean. What do they think is down there? Have they ever seen pictures? Emphasize the fact that there's a living world down there.

DURING
◄ In this exercise, you're going to pretend to be the diver, and the children are going to be all the things you see as you explore the underwater world.
◄ Explain this to the children and then "don" your scuba gear!
◄ Some of the things you might spot include the following:
  • A fish
  • An octopus
  • A sponge
  • The bubbles from your breathing
  • A sunken boat
  • A sea anemone (plant)
  • A shark
  • Barnacles
  • A jellyfish
  • A crab
  • An eel
  • Another diver

AFTER

- *Sand and water table and objects that sink or float*
- *Bubble mixture and wands*

◁ At the water table, provide a variety of materials and challenge the children to discover three that sink. (Make sure there are at least three possibilities.)

◁ Give the children blowing bubbles so they can simulate being underwater.

the Tide

BEFORE

◁ Tides occur twice a day and are caused by the unequal gravitational pull of the sun and the moon on different parts of the earth. Of course, this is a fairly technical explanation for young children. However, you can talk about high and low tides with the children and the fact that the sun and the moon affect them. Also discuss what waves look like from the beach during high and low tides. At high tide, waves tend to be larger—roaring in, cresting, and foaming as they approach the beach. During low tide, the waves don't come in as far and they're smaller, rolling in more gently, with just a few bubbles as they reach the sand.

DURING

◁ Ask the children to each move like a wave at low tide.

◁ Next, ask them to pretend that time is passing and the tide is getting higher. The waves continue to grow until, finally, at high tide, they're as big as they get.

◁ If time permits, reverse this process. Or you can begin with high tide instead.

ALSO

◁ Once the children have had the experience of acting as individual waves, you might want to try a group activity. To do this, divide the children into rows, one behind the other. The "waves" then work together to depict low and high tides.

AFTER

• *Sand and water table filled with water*
• *Water in sealed soda bottles*

◄ Ask the children to try and create tides at the water table. Or, put water in large empty soda bottles and invite them to experiment with low and high "tides."

Bodies of Water

BEFORE

◄ Ask the children if they know how rivers, lakes, and bays differ from each other and from the ocean? Discuss these bodies of water with them, pointing out as many characteristics as you can. For example, while a lake and bay could be the same size, a bay has salt water and is subject to tides, while a lake has fresh water and does not have tides. Therefore, a lake has less motion to it. A bay is smaller than the ocean. Also explain that rivers flow. Finally, explain the ways in which these bodies of water can be connected.

DURING

◄ Ask the children to choose what they want to pretend to be—a river, lake, bay, or ocean.

◄ Then tell them that you know a place where a river runs into and out of a small lake. Once the river comes out of the lake, it eventually runs into a bay, which is "around the corner" from the ocean. Can they show you what all of that would look like? (It will take some time and a lot of cooperation, but with some encouragement, they can do it!)

AFTER

• *"Down by the Bay" by Raffi (song or book)*

◄ Introduce the children to "Down by the Bay" from Raffi's *Singable Songs for the Very Young* or read Raffi's storybook, *Down by the Bay*.

Occupations

CHAPTER EIGHT

KEEPING HOUSE

Learning Objectives
• *To foster appreciation and respect for the occupation of homemaking*
• *To help eliminate gender stereotyping where homemaking is concerned*

BEFORE

◀ Talk to the children about how hard a job it is to be a homemaker and how keeping things clean and washed is just a part of the job. Ask them to tell you some of the things that need to be washed in a house.

DURING

◀ Ask the children to show you the movements involved in washing the following things. Be sure to stress realism. For example, explain that although the hand and arm movements involved in washing dishes may be similar to those required in washing a dog, the latter would occur at a different level in space. Similarly, washing dishes also calls for rinsing and the careful placement of those dishes in a drainer.

• Windows
• Dishes
• The floor
• The dog
• The bathtub
• A sink

AFTER

• *Paper plates, paper towels, empty cleaning bottles, and a mop*

◀ Put paper plates, paper towels, empty cleaning bottles, and a mop in the Housekeeping Center so the children can have additional washing experiences.

Preparing Meals

BEFORE

◄ Talk with the children about all the steps involved in preparing different kinds of meals. Some meals require chopping and stirring, while others call for mixing and pouring (for example, pancakes must be mixed, poured, and then flipped). Some foods are cooked in pans on the stove, others are baked in the oven, and some (such as salad) don't require any cooking at all. In addition, some dishes have complicated recipes that must be followed exactly, while others can be made from memory or experimentation!

DURING

◄ Ask the children to sing the following song with you (to the tune of "Here We Go 'Round the Mulberry Bush") while performing the action described. What other steps can they think of?

> **Preparing Meals**
> First we have to chop the food,
> Chop the food, chop the food.
> First we have to chop the food
> So we can eat our dinner.
>
> Now we have to mix it up,
> Mix it up, mix it up.
> Yes, we have to mix it up
> So we can eat our dinner.
>
> Now we have to pour the food,
> Pour the food, pour the food
> Now we have to pour the food
> So we can eat our dinner.
>
> Finally, we serve the food,
> Serve the food, serve the food.
> Finally, we serve the food
> And now we eat our dinner!

AFTER

• **Ingredients and equipment to prepare a meal with the children**

◄ Prepare an entire meal, from appetizers to dessert, with the children. Or simply place the appropriate materials in the Housekeeping Center so the children can "create" their own meals.

Taking Care of Clothes

BEFORE

◀ Clothes require a lot of care if they're going to remain clean and nice looking. Explain that some of the steps involved in taking care of clothes are washing them (some by hand, but most in a washing machine), drying them (on a line or in a dryer), ironing them, folding and putting them in drawers, or hanging them in closets.

DURING

◀ Separate the children into groups of four and ask each group to form a line, side by side.

◀ The first child in each line acts out washing the clothes, the second dries them, the third irons, and the fourth puts them away.

◀ Each child chooses how to perform his task.

◀ After the children have completed the four tasks, ask the group to rotate, with the last child going to the beginning of the line.

ALSO

◀ Once the children are familiar with this activity, you might want to introduce the musical elements of *accelerando* (gradually increasing the tempo) and *ritardando* (gradually decreasing the tempo).

◀ Start with a beginning tempo by clapping your hands at a medium slow pace. After every eighth clap, call out the word "change" or "switch" or "next" (or the name of the next task).

◀ Then, after each line of four children completes the washing process, increase the tempo of your clapping.

◀ When the children's actions have become as fast as you think is possible, reverse the process by decreasing the tempo until you're back to where you started.

AFTER
• Doll clothes, washbasin, and clothesline

◀ Put doll clothes, a washbasin, a clothesline, and other appropriate items in the Housekeeping Center so the children can practice washing clothes.

A Dusting Dance

BEFORE
- *Lively piece of music*
- *Pieces of cloth*

◄ Keeping a house dust-free is not an easy job, since all kinds of things tend to create dust (such as fireplaces and opening and closing doors). Also, there are so many things that have to be dusted—some things are way down low, and some are way up high, and some are tiny objects (such as knickknacks), which have to be lifted and dusted under. In addition, dusting can be bothersome because the dust can get in eyes and make them water or get in noses and cause sneezes.

◄ Choose a lively piece of instrumental music (for example, Mozart's "Eine Kleine Nacht Musik," a Strauss waltz, or a Top 40 favorite).

DURING

◄ Give each child a "dust cloth" (such as a chiffon scarf or a paper towel). Explain that they're going to turn dusting into a fun job by doing a dusting "dance."

◄ Put on the music you've selected and invite the children to "dust and dance," using their dust cloth in any way they like. (If necessary, to encourage creative use of space, remind the children that they have a whole house to dust and that they must bend and stretch to reach everything.) Is the dust tickling their noses? Are they using all the parts of their cloths? Of course, realism isn't as important as fun and creativity.

ALSO

◄ On subsequent repetitions of this activity, make it even more fun by asking the children what other body parts can hold their dust cloths!

AFTER
- *Dust cloths, feather dusters, and empty plastic bottles of furniture polish*

◄ Put dust cloths, feather dusters, and empty bottles of furniture polish in the Housekeeping Center.

Household Machines

BEFORE
• *Pictures of household machines, optional*

◄ In the "olden days," homemakers didn't have many machines to make their jobs easier. Fortunately, in modern times, there are more and more machines being invented to help homemakers.

◄ Ask the children to name any household machines they have at home or may have seen. How do they work? Show them pictures, if possible.

DURING
◄ Encouraging a variety of responses, ask the children to pretend to be each of the following:
  • Washing machine
  • Dryer
  • Vacuum cleaner
  • Electric can opener
  • Blender
  • Dishwasher
  • Coffee grinder
  • Coffee maker

ALSO
◄ Explain to the children that they're going to create a brand new machine. What housekeeping job do they think it should do? What would they like to call it?

◄ Begin by asking one child to repeatedly perform a movement that can be executed in one spot (such as jumping lightly in place or standing and reaching his arms toward the ceiling).

◄ A second child then stands near the first child and contributes a second movement that relates in some way to the first. For example, if the first child is performing an up-down motion by bending and stretching, the second child might choose to do the reverse, standing beside his classmate.

◄ A third child might choose an arm or leg motion that's timed to move between the two bodies bending and stretching.

◄ As these movements continue, each remaining child adds a functioning part to the machine. They may choose any movements they want, as long as they don't interfere with the actions of others and they contribute in some way to the machine. (You can even ask the children to perform sounds to accompany their motions!)

AFTER
• **Houses and Homes** *by Ann Morris*

◄ After the children have participated in all of these activities related to keeping house, introduce the concept of diversity among homes by reading Ann Morris' *Houses and Homes* with them.

The Nurse

BEFORE

◄ Have any of the children ever been in a hospital? If so, can they tell the rest of the group about the nurses? What kinds of things did they do?

◄ Talk to the children about nurses and how indispensable they are. Emphasize the responsibilities cited below, and explain that both men and women can be nurses.

DURING

◄ Ask the children to pretend to be nurses and act out the following duties:
  • Taking a temperature and reading the results
  • Giving a shot
  • Bringing a patient's meal
  • Listening to a heartbeat with a stethoscope
  • Writing information on a patient's chart
  • Dispensing medication
  • Taking a pulse

AFTER

• *Child-safe thermometer, stethoscope, "chart," and "medicine"*

◄ Place a child-safe thermometer, stethoscope, "chart," and "medicine" in the Dramatic Play Area so the children can continue their explorations of this profession.

The Mail Carrier

BEFORE

◄ Delivering mail to the correct addresses is an especially important job. Just think of what would happen if bills and letters from friends and loved ones were delivered to the wrong people or never delivered at all! For example, what if a child sent his grandmother a birthday card but she never got it? Grandma might feel forgotten and unloved!

◄ Discuss the meaning of the word *addressee.*

DURING

◄ Read the following poem to the children.

◄ Then ask them to pretend to be mail carriers as you read the poem again.

The Mail Carrier

The mail carrier totes the shoulder bag
With pride and care, because
Getting mail to its destination
Is the important work he does.

WEARING UNIFORMS

Learning Objectives
• *To familiarize the children with and enhance appreciation for occupations that usually require uniforms*
• *To foster appreciation for the individuality of the persons wearing the uniforms*
• *To help eliminate gender stereotyping with regard to certain occupations*

Driving the truck to the end of the street,
Then walking down one side;
Stopping at every mailbox there is
To deposit the mail inside.

She continues in this very same way,
Whistling a happy tune,
Pausing to say a friendly "hello"
And a pleasant "good afternoon."

So now the mail has all been delivered
To where it ought to be.
The sender can be sure of the mail
And so, too, can the addressee!

AFTER
• *Paper, pen or marker, and envelopes*

◀ Help the children write and address letters to someone—a parent or friend, perhaps.

The Firefighter

BEFORE
◀ Firefighting is an occupation that's particularly fascinating to children. To a child, the firefighter is a hero (with good reason!).
◀ Talk to the children about all the things firefighters do. Do any of the children want to be firefighters? Why?

DURING
◀ Ask the children to pretend to be firefighters and act out the following duties:
   • Slide down the pole
   • Run to the fire truck
   • Hold on tightly as the truck races to the fire
   • Get out the hose
   • Hose down the burning building
   • Chop through a wall with an ax
   • Climb the ladder
   • Return the equipment to the truck

ALSO
◀ You can also ask the children to pretend to be the all-important firefighting equipment. Ask them to depict the following:

- The fire pole
- A fire truck
- The ladder being extended
- The fire hose being unraveled
- The fire hose gushing water
- An ax breaking down a wall
- The ladder being lowered

AFTER
- **Curious George at the Fire Station by Margret Rey and H. A. Rey**

◀ Read Margret Rey and H.A. Rey's *Curious George at the Fire Station* to the children.

Waiting Tables

BEFORE
◀ Unlike nurses and firefighters, waiters and waitresses are not in the business of saving lives. But a good waitperson adds cheer to a diner's day and makes a good meal even better.
◀ Talk to the children about the tasks involved in waiting tables and how important it is to do good work, whatever the job.

DURING
◀ Teach the children the song below (sung to the tune of "This Old Man").
◀ Then sing it with them as they each pretend to be a waitperson. The children can act out any appropriate tasks they choose, based on your discussion. If they get stuck, you can offer reminders.
◀ Possibilities include:
- Taking the orders
- Carrying a heavy tray
- Lowering the tray carefully onto a stand
- Serving the meals
- Pouring water or coffee
- Removing the empty plates

◀ The lyrics of the song are as follows:

Waiting Tables
Waiting tables
Is what I do;
I will bring your meal to you.
With care and grace and a nice smile, too,
I will do my best for you.

AFTER

* *Play aprons, paper plates, utensils, tablecloths, and play food*

◄ Put aprons, paper plates, utensils, tablecloths, and play food in the Dramatic Play Area.

The Bell Captain

BEFORE

◄ People who stay in hotels would often be lost (sometimes literally!) without the valuable assistance of a bell captain. Four of the bell captain's responsibilities are mentioned in the little verse below.
◄ Talk to the children about these responsibilities and why they're so helpful to hotel guests.

DURING

◄ Ask the children to individually decide what action they'd like to perform—in place—for each of the lines in the following verse.
◄ After they have decided, they will stand in a row, side by side.
◄ Then, as you continuously recite the verse (slowly at first), each child in turn performs an action for the line being read. (You can go back and forth, moving down and up the line, or start again at the beginning of the line each time.)
◄ Gradually increase the pace until it's as fast as the children can handle.
◄ The verse is as follows:

> **The Bell Captain**
> *Open a door;*
> *Hail a cab.*
> *Give directions;*
> *Carry a bag.*

ALSO

◄ As another activity, ask the children to form a circle and start walking slowly around. Begin reciting the verse at a slow tempo, with the entire group performing every line together. Again, gradually increase the tempo.

AFTER

* *Bell, whistle, and suitcases*

◄ Create a "hotel" in the Dramatic Play Area. Put a bell, whistle, and suitcases in the area. The children's sleeping mats can serve as beds in the hotel rooms. Some children can be guests, while others are clerks and bell captains.

The Sculptor

BEFORE

◄ A sculptor is an artist who carves, molds, or shapes statues or figures from different materials. Sometimes the material is as hard as marble, which must be chiseled; sometimes it is as soft as clay, which must be molded. And sometimes the material is metal, which needs to be cut and shaped.

◄ If there is a well-known sculpture in your area, use it as an example for the children. Help them to understand that before the sculpture could exist, an artist known as a sculptor had to imagine, design, and create it.

◄ Also talk to them specifically about molding clay into a sculpture. Most of them have probably worked with clay and can describe what it's like.

DURING

◄ Divide the children into pairs. Explain that one child will be the sculptor and the other will be the clay.

◄ The "clay" starts as a lump on the floor.

◄ The "sculptor" then begins "working the clay" (by arranging the child's limbs and body parts), creating whatever final shape he desires.

◄ Once the task is complete, the children reverse roles.

◄ Stress that the sculptor must work gently with the clay, and that certain body parts and limbs can only move in certain directions.

AFTER

• *Clay or playdough*

◄ As a follow-up activity, give the children clay or playdough so they can create their own sculptures.

◄ Also, if there is a well-known sculpture in your area, bring the children on a field trip to see it. What can they tell you about its shape and design?

Learning Objectives
• *To foster appreciation for the contributions of visual and performing artists*
• *To help the children see the arts as an option when making career choices*

BEFORE

◀ Imagine a world without music! How sad a place the world would be if there were no music to listen and dance to.

◀ What kinds of music do the children like best? Why? Talk to them briefly about the instruments used to make different styles of music. For example, a rock band generally consists of singers, guitars, bass guitar, and drums. A "big band" includes those same instruments, as well as horns (saxophones, clarinets, trumpets, and trombones). An orchestra wouldn't be an orchestra without a piano, strings (violins, violas, and cellos), French horns, flutes, tubas, and percussion instruments (cymbals, gong, triangle, and so on).

◀ Ask the children, "If you were musicians, what instruments would you want to play?"

DURING

◀ Ask the children to pretend to be playing the following instruments:
- Guitar
- Piano
- Drums
- Flute
- Slide trombone
- Saxophone
- Violin
- Triangle
- Cymbals
- Trumpet
- Gong

ALSO

◀ Divide the children into groups of four or five and ask each group to form a "rock and roll band."

◀ Compulsory instruments are guitar, bass guitar, and drums. Optional elements are a saxophone player, keyboard player, and lead singer (although it's necessary to have at least one singer, instrumentalists can also act as singers).

◀ Another option is to create a "big band" or "orchestra" with the entire group.

AFTER
- *A variety of rhythm instruments*
- *Prokofiev's* Peter and the Wolf

◀ Place a variety of instruments in the Music or Dramatic Play Center. Also, listen to pieces such as Prokofiev's *Peter and the Wolf* and ask the children to identify the different instruments.

The Puppeteer

BEFORE
* *Hand puppets or pictures of hand puppets, optional*

◄ A puppeteer is someone who entertains with puppets—most often for children. Shari Lewis, with Lamb Chop the puppet, is one example. Present generations of children have the creations of the late, great Jim Henson with which to identify. Among these famous puppets are Kermit the Frog, Miss Piggy, Oscar the Grouch, and Big Bird.

◄ If you have examples or pictures of hand puppets and marionettes (puppets that are operated from above by strings or wires, and sometimes by a rod), show them to the children and talk about the differences. Otherwise, simply discuss them. Have the children ever seen a puppet show in person? What kinds of puppets were in it?

DURING
◄ Divide the children into pairs. One child will be the puppeteer and the other a puppet.

◄ Ask the "puppet" to sit on the floor in front of the "puppeteer."

◄ It is up to the puppeteer to "give life" to his puppet. Each puppeteer can decide what kind of puppet to operate and what kinds of movements that puppet will perform.

◄ After a while, ask the partners to reverse roles.

AFTER
* *Materials to create puppets*

◄ Create puppets with the children!

BEFORE

• *Slow classical piece of music and a Top 40 song*

◄ Talk to the children in general terms about different kinds of professional dancing. Ballet, for example, is a very old form of dance that is extremely structured and graceful. Tap dancing involves tapping out rhythms with the feet and requires tap shoes, which have little pieces of metal on the tips, toes, and heels that make the tapping sounds. Jazz dancing is also very rhythmic but involves the whole body, including the head, shoulders, and hips. Much of the dancing seen in upbeat music videos can be considered jazz dance.

◄ Because dance has suffered from gender stereotyping, it would be helpful if you discussed the role of the male in professional dance. Of course, children may have seen men dancing, either in person or in film. But you can also point out that, although both male and female ballet dancers must be very strong in order to execute the difficult steps, male ballet dancers must be especially strong to lift their female partners off the floor. Also, most famous tap dancers have been men.

◄ Choose both a slow, classical piece of music and a Top 40 song.

DURING

◄ Put on the classical piece you've chosen and ask the children to pretend to be ballet dancers.

◄ Then, put on the Top 40 song and ask them to pretend to be in a movie about the music. (Because the children are pretending to be dancers—and are not simply being asked to dance to the music—they shouldn't be any more self-conscious than when asked to pretend to be mail carriers, for instance. However, if you find that dancing still makes them uncomfortable, make a game of Statues out of the activity.)

ALSO

• *Bottle caps*

◄ Press two or three bottle caps onto the bottom of the children's sneakers and ask them to pretend to be tap dancers!

AFTER

• *Books about dancing or dancers, such as* **Ballerinas Don't Wear Glasses** *by Ainslie Manson;* **Boy, Can He Dance!** *by Eileen Spinelli; or* **Alvin Ailey** *by Andrea Davis Pinkney*

◄ Read *Ballerinas Don't Wear Glasses* by Ainslie Manson; *Boy, Can He Dance!* by Eileen Spinelli; or *Alvin Ailey*, the story of the late, great modern dancer/choreographer, by Andrea Davis Pinkney. All of these titles are appropriate for children ages four to eight.

An Artist's Life

BEFORE

◀ So far the children have acted out the roles of sculptor, musician, puppeteer, and dancer. But there are other professions that fall into the category of the arts, including the work of poets, writers, photographers, conductors, painters, actors, choreographers, and composers. The poem below deals with four of these professions.

◀ Talk to the children about all of the artists mentioned above, focusing particularly on writers, conductors, painters, and actors.

DURING

◀ Read the following poem to the children.

◀ Then ask the children to act out the verses as you read it more slowly a second time.

◀ As you recite the last verse, the children can pretend to be any artists they choose—even those not mentioned in the poem.

An Artist's Life

The writer sits with pen in hand
Putting words upon the pages,
Describing things that touch the heart
Of readers through the ages.

The conductor works with baton
Weaving patterns in the air,
Guiding musicians as they play
With both subtlety and flair.

The painter works in a studio
Using colors dark and bright,
Putting brush to canvas until
The images are just right.

The actor steps upon the stage
And begins to play a role;
The character requires all
Of the body, heart, and soul.

An artist's life is not easy,
But it can be lived with pride.
The work is done out of love
So the artist is satisfied.

AFTER

• **Writing materials, easel and art supplies, and conductor's batons**

◀ Make writing materials, easels and art supplies, conductor's batons, and a small stage (use a large hollow wooden block) available for the children.

The Building Trades

Learning Objectives
• *To call attention to and foster appreciation for a variety of jobs not previously covered*
• *To emphasize the importance of doing a job well*

BEFORE

◀ Without the building trades, we'd have no buildings or houses! Talk to the children about the roles of architects, carpenters, roofers, bricklayers, and painters, stressing the importance of doing good work. After all, if a building isn't well designed or constructed, it won't last very long, and people could even get hurt. (Although there are certainly others in the building trades, this activity focuses on some that the children can most easily relate to.)

DURING

◀ Ask the children to pretend to do the following tasks:
  • Design a house (on imaginary paper)
  • Carry two-by-fours
  • Hammer nails
  • Saw wood
  • Measure something
  • Check to see if a door is level
  • Carry shingles up a ladder
  • Lay bricks for a chimney
  • Paint the inside walls with a roller
  • Paint the inside trim with a brush
  • Paint the outside walls with a spray gun

AFTER

• ***Child-sized tools and pieces of wood***
• ***Construction paper and drawing supplies***

◀ Place child-appropriate tools, along with pieces of wood, in the Dramatic Play Center.
◀ Give the children construction paper and drawing supplies and encourage them to design their own houses.

The Teacher

BEFORE

◄ Teachers have one of the most important responsibilities in the world—to teach! They help people (mostly children) learn everything from the ABCs to algebra, from physical fitness to physics, from history to how to get along with others. Just about everything there is to know can be learned from a teacher.

◄ Do any of the children want to be teachers? What do they want to teach? Why?

DURING

◄ Before acting out the following poem, ask the children to decide what movement they each want to perform for the last two lines of the first and last verses.

◄ Then, as you read the poem slowly, the children perform the appropriate movements.

The Teacher

Writing on a chalkboard,
Reading from a book,
Being sure that not one child
Has been overlooked.

Working the computer,
Pointing at the map,
Giving kids a signal when
It's time to take a nap.

Playing the piano,
Teaching kids to sing;
Teachers know that learning is
The most important thing!

AFTER

• **Books about teachers, such as** The Best Teacher in the World **by Bernice Chardiet or** The Day the Teacher Went Bananas **by James Howe**

◄ Read *The Best Teacher in the World* by Bernice Chardiet or *The Day the Teacher Went Bananas* by James Howe to the children.

BEFORE

◄ Among the valuable services office workers perform are typing, answering the telephone, making appointments, greeting clients, taking notes, and filing.

◄ Talk to the children about each of these tasks. If you want, mention that both men and women are office workers.

DURING

◄ Ask the children to pretend to be office workers and do the following tasks:
- Answer the telephone and make a call
- Write a note
- Type a letter
- Check the appointment book; make a notation in it
- Look up a telephone number in the phone book
- File folders in the filing cabinet
- Straighten up his or her desk

ALSO

◄ As with the firefighting activity (see page 158), the children can also pretend to be the tools found in an office. Ask them to depict the following:
- A typewriter
- A pencil; a pencil writing
- A telephone
- A filing cabinet; a filing cabinet drawer sliding open and shut
- A phone book; the phone book pages being flipped
- A computer
- The water cooler

AFTER

- *Play telephone, notepaper and writing instrument, telephone books, and file folders*

◄ In the Dramatic Play Area, place such items as a telephone, notepaper and writing instruments, telephone books, and file folders.

The Mechanic

BEFORE

◄ Before the automobile was invented, there was no such thing as an auto mechanic. But today people would be lost without their vehicles and, because vehicles break down, they would also be lost without mechanics!

◄ Not only is the mechanic's work important because we need our cars, but we also need to be safe in our cars. If a mechanic doesn't do good work and something goes wrong with a vehicle, the people in it could be in danger!

◄ Ask the children to name some of the jobs mechanics do. Then talk specifically with them about the jobs listed below. (Doing the "tune-up" is wide open to individual interpretation. The responses should be interesting!)

DURING

◄ Ask the children to pretend to do the following:

- Lift the hood of a car
- Check the oil
- Test the blinkers and lights
- Test the horn
- Pump gas
- Change a tire
- Put air in the tires
- Tow a car
- Do a tune-up
- Wash the windshield
- Test drive a car

AFTER

- *Books about cars and mechanics, such* **The Car Trip** *by Helen Oxenbury or* **Truck Song** *by Diane Siebert*
- *"Beep Beep" by the Playmates*

◄ Read Helen Oxenbury's *The Car Trip* or Diane Siebert's *Truck Song* to the children.

◄ If you can find a copy of "Beep Beep," a song made popular by The Playmates in the 1950s, put it on and play a game of Follow the Leader as the song grows increasingly faster!

The Bank Teller

BEFORE

◄ Despite the presence of automated teller machines, we still need real bank tellers to make transactions for us—and to add a personal, friendly touch to those transactions.

◄ Have the children ever been in a bank? Do they know what a teller is? Do they know what he does? Do they know what a bank is for? After receiving their input (you'll probably get some wonderful responses to these questions), in the simplest of terms, explain deposits and withdrawals to them.

DURING

◄ This activity is based on the classic game Mother, May I? but it is a bit more complicated to go along with the topic.

◄ Ask the children to stand in a row, facing you, at the far end of the room (the "vault").

◄ You're going to be the "teller," and the children are going to represent the money. You will either "withdraw" from or make "deposits" to the vault.

◄ If you specify a withdrawal, the children will move forward (toward you); if you specify a deposit, the children will move backward.

◄ But there's more: In this game, you won't ask for baby steps or giant steps and so on. You're going to withdraw and deposit *dollars* and *cents,* and specific locomotor movements will represent the amounts. A single cent is a step; a dollar is a jump; and $100 is a hop. (For example, if you say you need to withdraw ten cents, the children will take ten steps toward you. If you say you're depositing $4, the children will take four jumps backward. And if you say you're depositing $500, the children will take five hops backward.)

◄ And, of course, before the children can move at all, they must ask, "Teller, may I?"

AFTER

• *Play money in different denominations*

◄ Place play money of various denominations in the Dramatic Play Area.

Transportation

FLYING THE SKIES

Learning Objectives
• *To familiarize the children with various methods of traveling the skies*

BEFORE

◄ When you think about flying the skies, airplanes come to mind first. Airplanes come in different sizes and shapes and, therefore, possess different characteristics. The Concorde, for example, is the fastest passenger jet in the world. A glider plane, on the other hand, has no engine so it's quite a bit slower; it's also quieter and more graceful than the Concorde. A large cargo plane carries large loads (even cars and trucks!) and is neither quick nor graceful nor quiet; in fact, the cargo in the plane probably gets a rather bumpy, noisy ride.

◄ Discuss this with the children. Also talk about the basics of taxiing into position for take-off, gaining speed on the runway, taking off, climbing to cruising altitude, leveling off, descending, landing, and taxiing to the arrival gate.

DURING

◄ Ask the children to pretend to be the following:
- A cargo plane
- The Concorde
- A glider plane

◄ Then ask them to pretend to be a passenger jet and do the following:
- Taxi out from the gate and into position
- Accelerate down the runway
- Take off
- Climb to cruising altitude
- Level off and continue toward the passengers' destination
- Descend
- Land
- Taxi to the gate

AFTER

- *Books about flying, such as* **Planes** *by Byron Barton,* **Flying** *by Donald Crews, and* **Planes** *by Anne F. Rockwell*

◄ If possible, take a trip to a local airport (large or small!).

◄ Read *Planes,* illustrated by Byron Barton, Donald Crews' *Flying,* and *Planes* by Anne F. Rockwell to the children.

BEFORE

◄ For as long as there have been "spaceships," children have been fascinated with them. Talk to the children about the exploration of space. Explain that shuttlecraft are launched (both with and without astronauts) to do things such as take pictures of the earth and other planets. This helps us to learn a lot about our solar system.

◄ Have the children ever watched a space launch on television? Talk to them about the countdown, the ignition of the shuttle boosters, the lift-off, and the landing. Then discuss the things an astronaut might see while traveling through the sky, and the element of weightlessness.

DURING

◄ Ask each child to pretend to be a spaceship on the launching pad.

◄ With as much drama as possible, count down from ten.

◄ The "spaceships" then blast off and begin their ascent into outer space.

◄ Once "in orbit," the children can pretend to be the astronauts. What are they doing inside the spaceship? What are they seeing while on their journey?

◄ The astronauts will then put their spaceships into a "holding pattern" while they venture out.

◄ After moving about weightlessly for a while, the astronauts return to their spaceships and bring them back to earth, landing them safely on the runway.

AFTER

- **Space Songs for Children** *by Tonja Evetts Weimer*

◄ Play selections from Tonja Weimer's *Space Songs for Children,* a cassette with twelve songs written from a child's perspective. The accompanying book offers suggestions for related activities to extend the ideas in each song. Place the tape in the Music Center so the children can listen whenever they want.

Up, Up, and Away

BEFORE
* *Picture of a hot air balloon, optional*

◄ Have the children ever seen a hot air balloon? (They have if they've seen *The Wizard of Oz!*) Show them a picture of one, if possible. Talk about the basket where the people stand and the large, brightly colored balloon that is shaped like a light bulb.

◄ Explain that the balloon must first be laid flat on the ground, and then a fan is used to open it up. It takes about five people to get it upright.

◄ Once upright, a fire is lit (the balloons use propane gas), which creates the hot air that gets the balloon going.

◄ A hole in the top of the balloon is then made larger or smaller to regulate speed and direction. Hot air balloons can only be launched on days when it is not too windy.

DURING

◄ Ask the children to lie on the floor and pretend to be hot air balloons lying flat on the ground.

◄ Tell them that a fan has started to blow, and they are slowly expanding (while still lying down).

◄ Once they are fully expanded, the hot air balloons are lifted upright and the fires are started.

◄ The balloons then rise slowly into the air, where they drift smoothly over the trees.

◄ After a while, reverse the entire process.

AFTER
* **The Great Balloon Race** *by Rosie Heywood*

◄ Read *The Great Balloon Race* by Rosie Heywood to the children.

Whirlybird

BEFORE
- *Picture of a helicopter, optional*

◄ *Whirlybird* is a nickname for the helicopter. Have the children ever seen one? Describe a helicopter to them and, if possible, show them a picture. Explain that sometimes the front of it is a glass bubble that surrounds the pilot, and it sits on two long runners that resemble skis. The propellers are on top and spin horizontally (rather than vertically, as on the wings of a plane), beginning slowly and gradually increasing speed as the helicopter prepares for take-off. The tail is long and reminiscent of a dragonfly.

◄ Unlike a plane, a helicopter doesn't need to take off down a runway because it lifts straight off the ground. It also has the ability to hover (since hovering is critical to the activity, discuss this concept with the children), and the ride is "bumpier" in a helicopter than in a plane.

DURING
◄ This activity will provide the children with experience in the movement element of bound (interrupted) flow.

◄ Begin by asking the children to imagine that they're helicopters preparing for take-off. Once the "helicopters" are airborne and moving about the "sky" (if necessary, remind the children that this is a bumpy ride!), you will occasionally (at random intervals) call out, "Hover!" The helicopters must then do exactly that until you call out "Proceed!"

◄ Vary the amount of time between commands to keep the children guessing!

ALSO
◄ You can also explore the element of shape by dividing the children into groups of at least three and asking each group to create the shape of a helicopter, including runners, body, propellers, and tail.

AFTER
- *Art materials, such as paper, markers, scissors, and glue*

◄ Encourage the children to create their own helicopters using a wide variety of art materials.

The Air Show

BEFORE

‹ At air shows, stunt pilots in special jet planes amaze their audiences with all
kinds of daredevil maneuvers. Talk to the children about the maneuvers
mentioned in the following poem.

‹ Has anyone in the group ever seen an air show? What was it like?

DURING

‹ Ask the children to act out the following poem, each pretending to be a stunt
pilot's plane.

The Air Show

Rising, rising into the sky,
Into the face of the sun—
Higher and higher and higher we fly,
The airplane and pilot as one.

Suddenly we turn upside down,
Flying backward through the air—
Now the nose is heading back toward the ground
As we make loopdy-loops with flair.

Leveling out, then rising once more,
Then cut the engine to dive—
Getting close enough to hear the crowd roar
As the engine sputters alive.

We rise and fall and rise again,
There's no other way to fly—
We dip and soar and fall into a spin,
Then speed away across the sky.

AFTER

• **Paper and art materials, such as crayons, sparkles, and glue**

‹ Make paper airplanes with the children. Encourage them to decorate the planes
for their own air show!

Canoeing

BEFORE

◄ Have the children ever seen a canoe? Do they know how a canoe is paddled? Talk to them about canoeing and what it would be like in both smooth and rough water.

◄ Describe *white water rapids* to them. They are a part of a river where the water moves very quickly (making it frothy and white) and the surface is usually broken by obstructions, such as rocks. To "shoot the rapids" in a canoe means to maneuver the boat through the rough water.

DURING

◄ This is a partner activity (two people per canoe) that requires cooperation.

◄ Ask the children to choose partners. Then ask them to stand one behind the other, facing the same direction, and pretend to share a single canoe.

◄ The forward child leads in terms of dictating the direction of movement. Otherwise, the following instructions can lend themselves to individual interpretation. Also, it isn't necessary for partners to always be "paddling" on the same side of the canoe.

◄ Ask the partners to pretend to do the following:
  • Carry the canoe to the edge of the water
  • Get the canoe into the water
  • Get into the canoe without tipping it over
  • Paddle around a lake
  • Paddle against a sudden, strong wind
  • Go fishing while the canoe drifts along
  • "Shoot the rapids"

AFTER
  • *Art materials, such as paper, markers, scissors, and glue*

◄ You can use this activity as a link to or jumping-off point for studies of Native Americans. Explain that most of today's canoes are made of fiberglass, but the Native Americans crafted theirs out of wood.

◄ Provide the children with art materials and encourage them to create their own canoes.

Learning Objectives
• *To familiarize the children with various methods of water travel*
• *To heighten awareness of the earth's water as a valuable resource*

CHAPTER NINE • *Transportation*

The Submarine

BEFORE
• Picture of a submarine, optional

◄ A submarine, which spends more time underwater than "riding the waves," is a form of water transportation for members of the military and oceanographers. By definition, a submarine is a "submersible ship."

◄ Talk to the children about subs and show them a picture, if possible. Describe the functions of the periscope and hatch, and talk about the commands listed below.

◄ This activity will not only call attention to submarines as a form of water transportation, but will also focus on the concepts of *up* and *down*.

DURING
◄ Ask the children to pretend to be submarines, moving along the surface of the ocean.

◄ Tell them that you are the commander, and as they travel about the ocean, they are to do as you say.

◄ The commands you can issue include the following:
  • Dive! (Submerge and continue to travel underwater)
  • Up periscope! (Once up, the periscope should swivel around in all directions)
  • Down periscope!
  • Surface! (Rise to the ocean's surface)
  • Open hatch! (This and the following command can only be issued when the sub is above water.)
  • Close hatch!

AFTER
• Map or globe of the world

◄ Explain to the children that submarines can only travel in the ocean. Why do they think that might be? Show the children a world map and point out all the oceans.

Row, Row, Row Your Boat

BEFORE

◄ "Row, Row, Row Your Boat" is a classic song typically sung in rounds. One person or group begins singing; at the conclusion of the first line, the second person or group joins in, beginning with the first line. Since there are only four lines, there can be only four rounds (individuals or groups). Explain this to the children.

◄ Also discuss the movement involved in rowing a boat, which is different from paddling a canoe.

◄ Divide the children into four groups and practice singing "Row, Row, Row Your Boat" in rounds. The lyrics are as follows:

Row, Row, Row Your Boat

Row, row, row your boat
Gently down the stream.
Merrily, merrily, merrily, merrily,
Life is but a dream.

DURING

◄ Once the children are comfortable with singing the song in a round, it's time to add movement to the song.

◄ Line up the groups at one end of the room, one behind the other, with the members of each group standing side by side. (Make sure they have enough elbow room for "rowing.")

◄ As the first group begins to sing, they start walking toward the other side of the room, making a rowing motion with their arms.

◄ The second group does likewise at the conclusion of the first line, and so on.

◄ When each group reaches the end of the room, the members can split up, half going to the right and half to the left, continuing the activity down the sides of the room. They can then meet in the middle and continue once more.

ALSO
• *Carpet squares*

◄ If you have the space and enough carpet squares to go around, you can exercise the children's legs at the same time that you familiarize them with rowing and rounds. Ask the children to sit on carpet squares, still singing and performing the rowing motion, but using their feet and legs to propel themselves forward.

AFTER
• *Recorded version of "Row, Row, Row Your Boat"*
• **Who Sank the Boat?** *by Pamela Allen*

◄ "Row, Row, Row Your Boat" is available on a number of recordings, including *Wee Sing Sing-Alongs*. Put the recordings in the Music Center.

◄ Read Pamela Allen's *Who Sank the Boat?* to the children.

BEFORE
* *Pictures of boats*

◁ This activity gives children the opportunity to experience the difference between pretending *to be* something and pretending *to do* something. Discuss the topics listed below, as well as the relationships between each *being* and *doing* pair. Also, show the children any pictures you have that can help make these images more clear.

◁ Explain that a kayak is a canvas-covered portable canoe. A double-bladed kayak paddle has a paddle on each end of the pole and is usually dipped alternately on either side of the boat.

DURING

◁ Ask the children to pretend to *be* and *do* the following.

◁ To fully experience the contrast, you should alternate from one column to the other (it doesn't matter which you do first). However, if you prefer, you can complete all of one column before doing the other.

* **Being**

  An anchor being raised
  An outboard motor
  The mast of a tall ship
  A double-bladed kayak paddle
  A life preserver
  A rubber boat being inflated

* **Doing**

  Raising an anchor
  Starting an outboard motor
  Climbing the mast of a tall ship
  Paddling a kayak
  Throwing out a life preserver
  Inflating a rubber boat

AFTER
* *Art materials, such as paper, markers, scissors, and glue*

◁ Provide a variety of art materials and encourage the children to create their favorite kind of boat.

◁ Take a vote to see which kind of boat is the most popular.

Smooth Sailing

BEFORE
• Picture of a sailboat, optional

◄ This activity lends itself to relaxation, as does the act of sailing itself. Have any of the children ever been on a sailboat? Did they find it peaceful?

◄ Talk about the terms and images in the following poem. If possible, show them a picture of a sailboat.

DURING

◄ Explain to the children that they are going to pretend to be the sails on a sailboat as you read the following poem (slowly and softly).

◄ They begin by lying "furled" upon the "deck." (Explain what this means.)

Smooth Sailing

Starting now to unfurl,
Rising slowly up the mast;
Stretching, stretching,
Open and free at last.

Gently pushed by the wind,
Billowing softly in the breeze;
Sailing, sailing
Over the peaceful seas.

Swinging right, swinging left,
Then heading back toward shore;
Falling, falling,
Lying on deck once more.

AFTER
• Variety of boats, and a sand and water table

◄ Place a variety of boats at the water table and challenge the children to discover how wind (their breath) can make the boats move.

DRIVING, RIDING, AND CYCLING

Learning Objectives
• *To familiarize the children with other types of transportation*

Traffic Lights

BEFORE
• ***Three large pieces of paper or cardboard (one red, one green, and one yellow)***

◄ Safety is an important issue where transportation, particularly driving, is concerned. Talk to the children about traffic lights. A red light means traffic must stop, and a green light means drivers can go through an intersection. A yellow light means to proceed with caution, because a red light is about to appear.

◄ For this activity, you'll need three large pieces of paper or cardboard—one red, one green, and one yellow.

DURING
◄ Explain to the children that they're going to pretend to drive cars or trucks.

◄ When they see a "green light" (when you hold up the green paper), they can go.

◄ Similarly, a "red light" means they must stop.

◄ At the "yellow light," they should walk in place.

ALSO
◄ You can use this activity as an opportunity to practice other motor skills. For example, a green light can indicate that the children should gallop. A yellow light can mean that they must hop in place, or substitute a nonlocomotor skill, such as twisting or shaking.

AFTER
• ***Blocks, toy cars, and toy trucks***

◄ Encourage the children to create their own roadways complete with traffic signs, using blocks or other materials. Place toy trucks and cars in the Dramatic Play Area and encourage the children to explore!

Bus Stop

BEFORE

◄ Have the children ever ridden on a bus? If so, they know that buses (both school buses and city buses) make frequent stops to let some passengers off and to pick up others. But the drivers don't stop just anywhere. There are designated bus stops along a route where people can get off and on.

◄ Designate three or four "bus stops" in your room, and determine where the bus "terminal" is going to be. That will be the spot where the "bus" begins and ends its daily route.

DURING

◄ Divide the children among the bus stops.

◄ Acting as the driver, begin your route by pausing at each of the bus stops to pick up passengers (the children get in line behind you).

◄ On your first trip around, all of the "passengers" should get on board. However, as you continue to make the rounds, passengers can get off and board the bus as they choose.

◄ When making your final round, deposit all the passengers at their original stops before you return to the terminal.

◄ As you operate the "bus," remember that sometimes buses go fast and sometimes slow. Sometimes they come to red lights (stop), and sometimes they get stuck in traffic (walk in place).

ALSO

◄ Once the children are familiar with this activity, they can take turns being the bus driver.

AFTER

◄ Sing "The Wheels on the Bus," encouraging the children to make up new verses.

BEFORE

◄ The bicycle is a nice, inexpensive, pollution-free way of getting around. How many of the children have bicycles? What's the farthest they've ever ridden?

DURING

◄ Teach the children the following song, sung to the tune of "A Bicycle Built for Two" (or "Daisy").

◄ Encourage them to sing it with you (or you can sing it to them) as they pretend to be cycling.

> ### Cycling
> *Riding, riding*
> *On my brand new bike.*
> *The carefree feel of gliding*
> *Is what I really like.*
> *I can pump up hills,*
> *I can coast down, too.*
> *I can ride without spills*
> *'Cause I know just what to do.*

ALSO

◄ You can also ask the children to show you the differences involved in riding the following:
  - A tricycle
  - A unicycle
  - A mountain bike
  - A racing bike
  - A tandem bike (built for two)
  - A moped

AFTER
- **Bicycle Race** *by Donald Crews*

◄ Read Donald Crews' *Bicycle Race* to the children.

All Aboard!

BEFORE

◀ Children today haven't had as much opportunity to experience trains as those in the past did. Have any of the children ridden on a train? What was it like? What was the longest train they ever saw?

◀ The following is another Follow the Leader activity, similar to Bus Stop (page 183), but it requires more cooperation among the children.

DURING

◀ Ask the children to choose partners. Each pair will pretend to be a two-car train (the child in back holds the waist of the child in front).

◀ Explain that as the "trains" travel about (being careful not to collide with one another), they should begin hooking onto each other, until eventually they've created one long train.

◀ As the trains move, call out various directions to vary the movement.

◀ The directions can include the following:

- You're going up a steep, steep hill
- You're coming down the other side
- You're stopping to pick up passengers
- Back up
- Gradually increase your speed

AFTER

- **Books about trains, such as The Little Engine that Could by Watty Piper or Train Song by Diane Siebert**
- **Train set, optional**

◀ Tell the children the story of *The Little Engine that Could,* or *Train Song* by Diane Siebert.

◀ If you have a train set available, set it up in the classroom.

Transportation Topics

BEFORE

◄ This activity covers a wide variety of people and things related to transportation, some of which have not been covered in other activities. Talk about them with the children, making sure all of the images are clear.

DURING

◄ Ask the children to pretend to be the following:
- A train engineer
- The doors on a bus
- A racecar driver
- The hood of a car
- The driver of an 18-wheeler
- A train whistle
- Bicycle spokes
- Tricycle handlebars
- A blinking traffic light
- The ice cream truck
- The wheels on a train
- Windshield wipers
- A railroad gate
- Railroad tracks

AFTER

- *Books about vehicles, such as* **Things That Go** *by Anne Rockwell*
- *Transportation toys and a box*

◄ Now would be a good time to read Anne Rockwell's *Things That Go,* which reviews trains, trucks, sailboats, buses, bicycles, and other forms of transportation.
◄ You can also place various transportation toys into a "feely box" and challenge the children to identify them.

Fun Themes!

Exploring Shapes

Learning Objectives
• To enhance body and spatial awareness
• To offer experiences with the movement element of shape
• To stimulate visual awareness
• To call attention to geometric, letter, and number shapes

BEFORE

◄ Sit with the children and ask them to look around the room, making note of the different shapes of the various objects in the classroom. Can they point out something that's round? Flat? Wide?

◄ Continue in this manner, covering (and discussing, if necessary) all the shapes listed below.

◄ Then select items in the room not yet pointed out, and ask the children to tell you what shapes they are.

DURING

◄ Ask the children to show you, with their bodies, the following shapes:
  • Round
  • Flat
  • Wide
  • Narrow
  • Pointed
  • Crooked
  • Angular
  • Long

◄ Now ask them to create, with their bodies, the shapes of different objects in the room. Possibilities include:
  • A desk
  • A chair
  • A pencil
  • A globe
  • The chalkboard
  • A book
  • A ruler

ALSO

◄ Combining shapes can make this activity much more challenging. For example, ask the children, alone or with partners, to create a shape that's both long and pointed, flat and round (such as a pancake), or wide and angular.

AFTER

• *Books about shapes, such as* My Very First Book of Shapes *by Eric Carle or* Pancakes, Crackers and Pizza: A Book of Shapes *by Marjorie Eberts*
• *Art materials, such as paper, markers, scissors, and glue*

◄ Read Eric Carle's *My Very First Book of Shapes* or Marjorie Eberts' *Pancakes, Crackers and Pizza: A Book of Shapes* to the children.

◄ Provide them with a variety of art materials so they can create their own shapes.

Imagining Shapes

BEFORE

◄ The previous activity (Exploring Shapes on page 188) requires the children to physically imitate what their eyes are seeing. With this activity, they'll use their "mind's eye." In other words, they will have to imagine how certain things look (things with which they're familiar but that are not right in front of them) and then create the appropriate shapes with their bodies.

◄ Listed below are objects typically found in the home that are likely to be familiar to the children. Feel free, however, to contribute ideas of your own. Just make sure to first talk with the children about the things you're going to ask them to create.

DURING

◄ Possible shapes to explore include the following:
  • A refrigerator
  • A water faucet
  • A dining room table
  • A couch
  • A teapot
  • A lamp
  • A telephone
  • A pillow
  • A rug

AFTER
• **Mr. Al Sings Colors and Shapes by Mr. Al**

◄ Choose selections from Mr. Al's *Mr. Al Sings Colors and Shapes* to play for the children. Then place the recording in the Music Center.

Changing Shapes

BEFORE
• *Music with a steady beat*

◄ If the children have experienced the two previous activities (Exploring Shapes and Imagining Shapes), then they know that their bodies can assume a wide variety of shapes.

◄ Simply reinforce that fact and further explain that bodies can create different shapes while remaining in one spot, as well as while moving around.

◄ Choose a piece of music with a steady 4/4 beat (for example, many Top 40 and rock-and-roll songs are written in 4/4) that easily lends itself to walking.

DURING

◄ Ask the children to walk around the room while the music is playing, explaining that you'll be asking them to change their bodies' shapes as they walk.

◄ Do this simply by calling out the shape you want them to assume. (Be sure to give them enough time to experience one shape before calling out another.)

◄ In addition to shapes already explored, possibilities include:
- Big
- Small
- Skinny
- Tall
- Lopsided
- "Funny"

AFTER

- **Books about shapes, such as Is It Larger? Is It Smaller? and Shapes, Shapes, Shapes, both by Tana Hoban**

◄ Read other books about shapes such as Tana Hoban's *Is It Larger? Is It Smaller?* and *Shapes, Shapes, Shapes.*

BEFORE

- **Alphabet chart, or blackboard and chalk**

◄ Review the letters of the alphabet with the children. Point them out on a chart or write them on the blackboard.

◄ Point out that some letters are made of straight and zigzagging lines, some of curved lines, and some of both.

DURING

◄ Choose letters that can be easily formed by the body, and ask the children to form them.

◄ Possibilities include the letters I, O, T, C, X, Y, L, Q, S, U, and V. (The children may choose to form either upper- or lowercase letters.)

ALSO

◄ You can also ask the children to choose partners and form letters in pairs. Possibilities include T, X, Y, J, Q, V, W, Z, A, D, P, R, H, J, K, N, and M.

◄ A second alternative, if the children are experienced enough, is to ask groups of children to create short words with their bodies (for example, S-O, H-I, or L-I-P).

◄ Finally, you can ask the children (alone or with partners) to form the shapes of numbers.

AFTER

- **"Marching Around the Alphabet" by Hap Palmer**

◄ One of the songs on Volume I of Hap Palmer's *Learning Basic Skills Through Music* is "Marching Around the Alphabet." Play it for the children and then place it in the Music Center.

Geometric Shapes

BEFORE
- *Pictures of geometric objects, or actual objects*

◄ Using pictures or actual objects as examples, discuss basic geometric shapes, such as circles, triangles, squares, and rectangles. Ask the children to tell you how these shapes differ.

DURING

◄ Separate the children into groups of three.

◄ Then, as you sing each of the following verses (to the tune of "I'm a Little Teapot"), each group forms the appropriate geometric shape.

Geometric Shapes

I'm a little circle,
Round as can be.
My lines are curving—
Look at me!

I am a triangle
With three sides;
I can be narrow
Or I can be wide!

Now it's a square
That you will see.
It takes four sides
For a square to be!

Look at the rectangle—
Four sides, too.
I can change my
Shape just for you!

AFTER
- *Books about shapes, such as* **Circles, Triangles, and Squares; Cubes, Cones, Cylinders & Spheres;** *and* **Shapes, Shapes, Shapes** *all by* **Tana Hoban**

◄ Read the children Tana Hoban's *Circles, Triangles, and Squares; Cubes, Cones, Cylinders & Spheres;* and *Shapes, Shapes, Shapes.*

How Deep Is the Ocean, How High Is the Sky?

BEFORE

◄ Ask the children what things they think of when you mention the color blue. Chances are their lists will include water and the sky.

◄ Talk about the different shades of blue they've seen in the ocean or the sky. Then ask them to tell you how deep they think the ocean is and how high they think the sky is.

◄ This activity calls attention to the color blue and deals with the concepts of *high, middle,* and *low* as well as *up* and *down*.

DURING

◄ Now ask the children to show you how deep the ocean is and how high the sky is. How much distance is there between the bottom of the ocean and the sky? Where, in relation to the ocean's bottom and the sky, would they place the ocean's surface? Can they show you with their bodies?

◄ Explain that you're going to be calling out three words—*bottom, surface,* and *sky.* When they hear one of those words, they are to show you with their bodies where the bottom, surface, and sky are in relation to one another. (If necessary, you can get more explicit by using the terms *low, middle,* and *high*.)

◄ Begin calling out these words, in any order, at a slow tempo. As the children catch on, start picking up the tempo until it's as frenzied as you want it to get.

◄ Then slow it down again. You can also mix the tempos, keeping the children unprepared for what's going to happen next. For example, you might move quickly from bottom to surface, and then very slowly to sky.

◄ In addition, you can mix up the order in which you say the words, sometimes skipping one and sometimes repeating the same one.

AFTER

◄ Bring the children outdoors on a number of different days to look at the sky. How would they describe its color from day to day?

◄ Also, if you have a body of water of any kind nearby, take a field trip! How does the blue of the water differ from the blue of the sky, if at all?

Mellow Yellow

BEFORE

◄ Yellow is a reminder of many pleasant things, such as flowers, the sun, butter, bananas, and lemon sherbet, to name a few.

◄ What do the children think of when you mention the color yellow? Talk about the examples they cite, including the shape of each one.

DURING

◄ Ask the children to show you the *shape* of each of the following yellow things.
  - The sun
  - A lemon
  - A school bus
  - A banana
  - A dandelion
  - A diamond-shaped road sign
  - A pat of butter, a stick of butter, and a tub of butter

◄ Now ask them to pretend to *be* the following yellow things:
  - A bumblebee
  - A blinking yellow traffic light
  - A school bus
  - The sun shining
  - A lemon being squeezed
  - A sunflower swaying in the breeze
  - Butter being spread

AFTER

- ***Books about colors, such as* Of Colors and Things *by Tana Hoban or* Little Blue and Little Yellow *by Leo Lionni.***

◄ Read Tana Hoban's *Of Colors and Things* or Leo Lionni's *Little Blue and Little Yellow*.

It's Not Easy Being Green

BEFORE

◄ "It's not easy being green," sings Kermit the Frog. His point is that because so many things in nature are green, he doesn't stand out.

◄ Ask the children to name some things that are green, and talk about each one.

◄ Then explain that when Kermit starts this famous song (play it if you have it!), he's wishing he were a different color. However, by the end of the song, he has realized that green is a wonderful color to be.

DURING

◄ Ask the children to stand in a circle, with a bit of space between them.

◄ Then move around the outside of the circle, touching each child and assigning him to be something green. (Use some of the children's examples or the possibilities listed below.)

◄ Assign one child to be "frog" (or "Kermit") and trade places with him.

◄ Now you assume the shape of a frog at your place within the circle, and the child moves like a frog around the circle, making the "assignments."

◄ When he selects another child to be a frog, they also change places. The game continues until all the children in the circle have been turned into frogs.

◄ Possible green things include:
  • A leaf
  • A blade of grass
  • A pickle
  • A head of lettuce
  • A pine tree
  • A dollar bill

ALSO

• *Scraps of green paper, marker, and a container*

◄ This activity can point out just how wrong Kermit was when he thought a frog couldn't be noticed among all the other green things in nature.

◄ Write the names of green things (see list above) on scraps of paper, and place them into a container. (Put in one scrap of paper with the word *frog* on it.)

◄ Choose one child to be the "guesser." That child then either leaves the room or stands aside, with his eyes closed and ears covered, while the rest of the children draw papers.

◄ These children then quickly take on the shapes they've drawn.

◄ When they're ready, ask the guesser to open his eyes and try to identify which child is the "frog." The object is for the guesser to do this as quickly as possible.

◄ Once identified, the frog becomes the guesser, and the game continues.

AFTER

• *"It's Not Easy Being Green" and/or "Colors" by Hap Palmer*

◄ If you have this song of Kermit's, place it in the Music Center. Also, Hap Palmer does "Colors" on Volume I of *Learning Basic Skills Through Music,* and "Parade of Colors" on Volume II.

Hot and Cold Colors

BEFORE

◄ Ask the children how the color red makes them feel. Does it bring heat to mind? What about the color blue? Does it make them think of the cold?

◄ Discuss some of the reasons why red and blue bring hot and cold to mind. For example, flames and fire trucks are mostly red. And blue is the color that lips can turn when someone's been in the cold too long, perhaps in the cold blue ocean.

DURING

◄ Encourage the children to show you their own individual interpretations as they pretend to be the following:
  • Red-hot barbecue coals
  • Ocean waves
  • A sizzling fire
  • A blue Popsicle

◄ Now ask them to show you how the following make their bodies react.
  • Running into the cold ocean
  • Touching a red-hot stove
  • Jumping into a cold swimming pool
  • Walking under a red-hot sun
  • Being out in the cold too long

AFTER

• *Books about colors, such as* **Is It Red? Is It Yellow? Is It Blue?** *by Tana Hoban*

◄ Read Tana Hoban's *Is It Red? Is It Yellow? Is It Blue?* to the children.

Primary Colors

BEFORE
• *Crayons, markers, or paints and paper; or pictures in a book*

◄ *Primary colors* are defined by *Webster's Third New International Dictionary* as "any of a set of colors from which all other colors may be derived." Traditionally, the primary colors are red, yellow, and blue. Red and yellow combine to make orange, yellow and blue combine to make green, and red and blue combine to make purple.

◄ Talk to the children about primary colors and their combinations.

◄ Better yet, show them using crayons, markers, paints, or pictures in a book.

DURING
◄ Divide the class into three groups and assign each group a primary color.

◄ Ask each group (either in turn or all at the same time) to pretend to be as many different things in their color as they can think of.

◄ They can perform these examples individually or with other members of the group.

◄ Offer suggestions if the children need help. For the yellow group, suggest those things listed in Mellow Yellow (page 193). For the red and blue groups, possibilities include the following:

• **Red**
An apple
A fire engine
A strawberry
Hot coals
The planet Mars
A rose
A heart

• **Blue**
The ocean
The sky
A bluebird
A blueberry
The blue lines on notebook paper
A police officer's uniform
The flashing light on a police car

ALSO
◄ Assign one child from each group to pair up with a child from a different group

to "combine colors." Each pair must then depict something in the color they've created. For example, if a child from the red group and a child from the blue group pair up, they should create something purple. You can ask one pair at a time to do this (demonstrating for the rest of the class) or you can ask all of the pairs to work simultaneously.

◀ If the children need help, offer them suggestions. Possibilities for green can be found in It's Not Easy Being Green (page 194). Possibilities for the orange and purple pairs include:

- **Orange**

  An orange

  A ladybug

  A monarch butterfly

  A carrot

  Orange juice

- **Purple**

  A grape or bunch of grapes

  A plum

  An eggplant

  A pansy

  Lilacs

AFTER
- **Paints or markers and paper**

◀ Give the children paints or markers in the primary colors and challenge them to discover two that, when combined, create a third color. Can they do it again, but with a different color?

THE CIRCUS

Learning Objectives
- *To stimulate the imagination*
- *To have fun!*

Everybody Loves a Clown

BEFORE

◁ Probably nobody loves a clown more than a child because children love to laugh. Clowns come in all shapes and sizes (just like other people), but there are some things you can pretty much count on with all clowns. Can the children tell you what those things are?

DURING

◁ Explain to the children that they are going to pretend to be circus clowns. Ask them to do the following things. (The last suggestion is wide open to individual interpretation, giving the children a chance to "clown around" any way they want.)
- Walking around in big floppy shoes
- Honking his red nose
- Juggling
- Riding a unicycle
- Riding a unicycle and juggling at the same time
- Jumping on the trampoline (sometimes high; sometimes low)
- Entertaining the audience

AFTER

- ***Face paints and books about clowns, such as* You Think It's Fun to Be a Clown! *by David A. Adler***

◁ Help the children create clown costumes, face paint with them, and read them David A. Adler's *You Think It's Fun to Be a Clown!*

198

The Tightrope Walker

BEFORE

◄ After clowns, one of the most common images of the circus is the tightrope, also known as the high wire. This one piece of rope or wire is the focus of quite a lot of excitement under the "big top."

◄ Have any of the children ever seen a tightrope act? How do they think a tightrope walker gets from one side to the other without falling off? Balance is the key! What do the children think it means to have good balance?

DURING

• Chalk or masking tape

◄ Create a "tightrope" on the floor with chalk or masking tape (unless you already have a straight line running across the floor that will serve the purpose).

◄ Then tell the children to pretend to be tightrope walkers making their way across the high wire. (You may want to assure them there's a net below!)

◄ Once each child has crossed successfully, challenge him to try it sideways and then backward.

◄ Are there any other ways they can move across the tightrope without stepping off?

AFTER

• Books about tightrope walkers, such as Mirette on the High Wire by Emily McCully

◄ Read Emily McCully's *Mirette on the High Wire* to the children.

BEFORE
• *Picture of a stilt walker, optional*

◄ Have the children ever seen anybody walk on stilts? Describe it as best you can or, if possible, show the children a picture. What do they think it would be like to walk on such tall sticks and be up so high?

◄ Talk about the sensations and images mentioned in the following poem.

DURING

◄ Ask the children to pretend to be stilt walkers at the circus as they act out the following poem.

◄ The last two lines lend themselves to exploration. What kinds of "tricks" do they think could be performed on stilts?

Stilt Walkers
Up so high upon my stilts,
The ground so far below;
I can sway and I can tilt,
But I won't fall, you know.

It takes time, but I can turn
With lots of little steps.
There's no need to be concerned—
I've got a lot of pep!

With giant steps I can go
Around the circus grounds
Saying hi to those I know,
The acrobats and clowns.

And at the end of a day
Of walking on two sticks,
It is time for me to play
With learning some new tricks!

AFTER
• *Dolls and stuffed animals, Popsicle sticks, and rubber bands*

◄ Provide the children with a variety of dolls and stuffed animals, along with Popsicle sticks and rubber bands, so they can continue with their fantasy play.

The Flying Trapeze

BEFORE

◄ Many circus acts take place high above the ground: stiltwalking, the tightrope, and the trapeze act.

◄ Have any of the children ever seen a trapeze act—in person or on television? Discuss it in as much detail as possible, using such terms as *forward, backward,* and *swinging.* Also discuss the other concepts mentioned in the song below.

◄ Swinging is one of the six qualities of movement. This motion takes the form of an arc or a circle around a stationary base. It generally requires impulse and momentum, and can be executed by the body as a whole; by the upper or lower torso alone; and by the head, arms, and legs.

◄ Trapeze artists hold on with their arms, so the swinging they do uses the rest of their bodies. For the children, what's important is that they experience the "letting go" required of a swinging motion.

DURING

◄ Ask the children to pretend to be trapeze artists as you sing the following song, sung to the tune of "The Man on the Flying Trapeze."

The Flying Trapeze

Swinging so high on the flying trapeze
Forward and backward with the greatest of ease
I can't imagine anything that's more fun
This is the best job under the sun!
Forward I swing, then backward I fly
Performing for thousands up here so high
I hear them gasp when I dare to let go
Then grab hold again—it's part of the show!
It feels like I'm soaring as I swing to and fro
I wave to the fans, all smiling below
Then swing to my platform where I give a bow
That's the end of my swinging—but only for now!

AFTER
• **Any version of "The Man on the Flying Trapeze"**

◄ Teach the children to sing this song. If possible, find a recording of the original song "The Man on the Flying Trapeze" to play for them.

Ringmaster

BEFORE

◀ The ringmaster has a number of duties, most of which are performed in the center of the ring. Review all of the circus activities already explored, and talk about any others you and the children can think of. (If possible, exclude animals because they really don't belong in a circus setting.)

DURING

◀ This is a variation of a game called Punchinello, with which you and the children may already be familiar. In that game, one child ("Punchinello") stands in the center of a circle with the others all around. The other children then chant a rhyme, asking Punchinello what he can do. Punchinello shows them, they proclaim in rhyme that they can do it too, and then they do it.

◀ This activity is the same, except that the child in the center will be called "Ringmaster." (Change the words in the rhyme from "Punchinello" to "Ringmaster.")

◀ The movement that the child in the center performs should be something seen at a circus.

◀ A new ringmaster then enters the ring, and the chant is repeated.

◀ The chant is as follows:

> **Ringmaster**
>
> *What can you do, Ringmaster, Ringmaster?*
> *What can you do, Ringmaster, you? (The child in center demonstrates an action.)*
> *We can do it, too, Ringmaster, Ringmaster.*
> *We can do it, too, Ringmaster, you! (And the rest of the children do it!)*

AFTER

• **Pictures of circus things**
• **Tape or rope to form a circle (ring)**

◀ Place pictures of circus things around the room. Then, create a circle using tape or a rope ("the circus ring") where children can continue their role playing as ringmasters.

Giants and Elves

Learning Objectives
* To stimulate the imagination
* To have more fun!

BEFORE
* *Pictures of giants and elves, optional*

◄ Talk with the children about giants and elves. Most children are probably familiar with giants, but do they know what elves are?

◄ If possible, show the children a picture of both giants and elves and compare and contrast the differences between them.

◄ Read the following poem to the children, discussing such words as *bellow, scurry, dwell,* and *harmony.*

DURING

◄ Ask the children to pretend first be giants and then elves as you read the poem once again (much slower this time).

◄ For the last two lines, they can go from being one to being the other.

Giants and Elves
See the giants, great and tall
Hear them bellow, hear them call.
Life looks different from up so high
With heads and shoulders clear to the sky.
And at their feet they can barely see
The little people, so very tiny
Who scurry about with hardly a care,
Avoiding enormous feet placed here and there.
But together they dwell, the giants and elves
In peace and harmony amongst themselves!

ALSO

◄ Once the children are familiar with this poem and are able to perform it cooperatively, ask half of them to be giants and the other half to be elves. How do they want to display dwelling "in peace and harmony amongst themselves"?

◄ Repeat the activity immediately to give the children a chance to swap roles, or be sure they get to act out the opposite role the next time you read the poem.

AFTER
* *Books about giants and elves, such as* **Jack and the Beanstalk** *and* **Teeny Tiny,** *both retold by Jill Bennett*

◄ Read *Jack and the Beanstalk* or *Teeny Tiny,* retold by Jill Bennett and illustrated by Tomie dePaola, to the children.

◄ Ask them to compare other things that are very big and very small. Can they come up with ideas that fall into the same category? For example, giants are huge and elves are tiny. What are some huge and tiny animals (for example, a mouse and an elephant), or huge and tiny green, growing things (for example, a blade of grass and an evergreen tree)?

Dinosaurs

BEFORE
• *Pictures of dinosaurs*

◀ The following activity familiarizes the children with such important quantitative concepts as *big, small, heavy, light, medium, high, low,* and *between,* while also offering them experience with the movement elements of force and time.

◀ Show the children pictures of dinosaurs, pointing out the differences in their sizes. Explain that some walked very high and on two feet, while others were smaller and much lower to the ground. And others were somewhere in the middle—medium-sized.

◀ Tell the children that some dinosaurs were extremely large and weighed a great deal. And, although we don't tend to think much about small dinosaurs, some were indeed very small. In fact, one was only one meter (about 3 feet) tall! These dinosaurs weighed much less and had to be very quick to stay out of the way of the larger dinosaurs.

DURING
◀ Present the following challenges to the children:
- Show me how high you can get (like the biggest dinosaurs).
- Make yourself as big and heavy as you possibly can.
- Demonstrate what a medium-sized dinosaur would look like.
- Show me what an even smaller dinosaur would look like.
- Now show me the smallest dinosaur—one that moves very lightly.
- Make yourself as small as you possibly can—as though you are hiding from the dinosaurs!

ALSO
◀ Ask the children to move about the room in a scattered formation.

◀ When you call out the words "large and heavy," they should move like dinosaurs fitting this description.

◀ When you call out "quick and light," they should move accordingly.

◀ Vary the amount of time between calls so the children never know when to expect the next challenge.

AFTER
• *Books and poems about dinosaurs*

◀ Read *Chickens Aren't the Only Ones* by Ruth Heller to the children. (Dinosaurs laid eggs, too!) You can also read "Pachycephalosaurus," a poem by Richard Armour, found in *Sing a Song of Popcorn: Every Child's Book of Poems* by Beatrice Shenk De Regniers, et al.

Insects and Arachnids

BEFORE
- *Pictures of insects, optional*

◄ Children have a fascination with bugs. Ask them to name as many as they can, comparing and contrasting the examples they present. For example, some insects and arachnids walk (spiders), some fly (bees), and some crawl (worms and caterpillars). Some have wings (flies), while others have many legs (centipedes). Some are small (fleas) and some are large (giant moths). Some are cute (ladybugs) and some not so cute (tarantulas).

◄ Talk about these characteristics and those listed below. Show them pictures if you have them.

DURING

◄ Ask the children to demonstrate the following:
- An ant carrying food to the nest
- A caterpillar crawling
- A flea jumping
- A spider weaving a web
- A bee flying from flower to flower
- An inchworm moving along
- A mosquito buzzing
- A fly rubbing its front legs together
- A butterfly floating through the air

AFTER
- *Books and songs about insects*

◄ There are plenty of activities for this popular topic. You can play selections from Jane Murphy's *Songs About Insects, Bugs and Squiggly Things* and place it in the Music Center for repeated listening. Sing the "Eensy, Weensy Spider" with the children. Read Eric Carle's *The Very Busy Spider* and/or *The Very Hungry Caterpillar*.

◄ And, of course, you should go outdoors to discover and observe insects! Record your findings.

BEFORE
- *Pictures of fairies, optional*

◄ Certainly the most famous fairy of all time is Tinkerbell, Peter Pan's little friend. Are the children familiar with this story?

◄ In general, fairies are supposedly magical creatures that look like humans but are very tiny (only a few inches high). Some, like Tinkerbell, can fly, and most are very playful. Fairies are also sometimes called brownies, gnomes, pixies, and sprites.

◄ Show the children a picture of fairies, if possible. Discuss any unfamiliar terms in the poem below.

DURING

◄ Encourage the children to make themselves as small as possible and take on the characteristics of a fairy. Read the following poem as the children act it out.

> *Fairies*
>
> *A brownie, a pixie, a gnome, or a sprite—*
> *The fairy and her magic take flight.*
> *Her wings are transparent,*
> *Her body is light,*
> *Sprinkling fairy dust*
> *On all that's in sight!*

AFTER
- *Art materials, such as paper, markers, scissors, and glue*
- *Fairy tales*

◄ Give the children a variety of art materials and encourage them to create their own magic fairies.

◄ Then read the children a fairy tale!

Teddy Bears

BEFORE

◄ Children adore stuffed animals—perhaps teddy bears most of all. How many of the children have (or have ever had) a teddy bear? What things do they like best about teddy bears?

◄ Ask them to describe teddy bears to you, and list the words they use on a board or flipchart.

DURING

◄ Using the words the children used to describe teddy bears, ask them to show you, with their bodies, what those words mean.

◄ You may find some of the words they use below; if not, add them to the list!
- Snuggly/cuddly
- Soft
- Warm
- Squishy/squeezable
- Floppy/droopy
- Fun!

ALSO
- **_Recording of "Teddy Bears' Picnic"_**

◄ Ask the children to show you how teddy bears walk. How would they dance? How would they march?

◄ Play a recording of "Teddy Bears' Picnic" and ask the children to march to it as though they were teddy bears.

AFTER
- **_Books about teddy bears_**

◄ Read the children a book about teddy bears, such as _The Teddy Bears' Picnic_ by Jimmy Kennedy, _This Is the Bear_ by Sarah Hayes, _Corduroy_ by Don Freeman, and _Teddy Bears Stay Indoors_ by Susanna Gretz.

◄ Ask the children who have teddy bears or other stuffed animals at home to bring them in, and then hold a picnic of your own!

Index

Transition Tips and Tricks

For Teachers

Jean Feldman

The author of the best-selling book *Transition Time* brings you
more attention-grabbing, creative activities that provide
children with an outlet for wiggles,
while giving their brains a jump start
with cross-lateral movement games.
Catch their attention with songs, games,
and fingerplays for any time of the day.
These classroom-tested ideas are sure to
become favorites! 216 pages.

ISBN 0-87659-216-7

Gryphon House

Paperback

16728

Making Make-Believe

Fun Props, Costumes, and Creative Play Ideas
MaryAnn F. Kohl

Explore the world of make-believe with fun and easy-to-make props and costumes. *Making Make-Believe* offers storybook play, games, cooking, mini-plays, dress-up costumes, puppet ideas, and more to enrich children's play. Unlock the imaginations of young children, allowing them to create their own dramatic play experiences.

ISBN 0-87659-198-5

Gryphon House

Paperback

19674

The Big Messy* Art Book

*But Easy to Clean Up
MaryAnn F. Kohl

Bring the joy of creativity, the delight of imagination, and the thrill of an art adventure to young children. *The Big Messy Art Book* opens the door for children to experience art on a grander, more expressive scale. Paint a one-of-a-kind masterpiece from a swing, or try painting a ball while it moves! Children will dive into these big experiences in creativity and remember them with enthusiasm and pride. With *The Big Messsy Art Book*, you are giving them the opportunity to go beyond the ordinary and into the amazing!

ISBN 0-87659-206-X

Gryphon House

Paperback

14925

Block Play

The Complete Guide to Learning and Playing with Blocks
Sharon MacDonald

Create craft board trees, railroad tracks, and skyscrapers and watch children experience the joy of learning through blocks! Clear descriptions of what children learn by playing with blocks accompany the activities. Each activity is written to take into account the ability and interest level of the children and to encourage developmental skills such as problem solving, math, science, language, and social skills. *Block Play* is a must-have for every teacher. 192 pages.

ISBN 0-87659-253-1

Gryphon House

Paperback

19327

ALSO AVAILABLE FROM
SHARON MACDONALD

Everyday Discoveries

Squish, Sort, Paint & Build

Playing to Learn

Activities and Experiences that Build Learning Connections
Carol Seefeldt

Create meaningful experiences that engage children in learning through play. *Playing to Learn* uses age-appropriate activities to demonstrate how children learn by playing games, playing with each other and in small groups, listening to stories, and much more. *Playing to Learn* gives you hundreds of activities to make learning fun!

ISBN 0-87659-263-9

Gryphon House

Paperback

19325

Creating Readers

Over 1000 Games, Activities, Tongue Twisters, Fingerplays, Songs, and Stories to Get Children Excited about Reading
Pam Schiller

Explore the basic building blocks of reading with *Creating Readers,* the comprehensive resource that develops a strong foundation for pre-readers. *Creating Readers* gives teachers and parents the tools to teach pre-reading skills with more than 1000 games, activities, fingerplays, songs, tongue twisters, poems, and stories for the letters of the alphabet. This valuable resource develops the child's desire to read as well as the skills needed to begin reading. *Creating Readers* starts children ages three to eight toward a future rich with books and reading. 448 pages.

ISBN 0-87659-258-2 /

Gryphon House

Paperback

16375

Available at your favorite bookstore, school supply store, or order from Gryphon House at 800.638.0928 or www.gryphonhouse.com.

The Complete Resource Book

An Early Childhood Curriculum
Over 2000 Activities and Ideas
Pam Schiller and *Kay Hastings*

The Complete Resource Book is an absolute must-have book for every teacher. Offering a complete plan for every day of every week of the year, this book is an excellent reference book for responding to children's specific interests.

Each daily plan contains: circle time activities, music and movement activities, suggested books, and six learning center ideas. The appendix is jam-packed wih songs, recipes, and games. *The Complete Resource Book* is like a master teacher working at your side, ofering you guidance and inspiration all year long.

ISBN 0-87659-195-0

Gryphon House

Paperback

15327